Simple
NOT EASY

A Way of Being

ELLEN BONE

Edited by Lil Barcaski

Published by: GWN Publishing
www.GWNPublishing.com

Cover Design: Kristina Conatser

ISBN: 978-1-965971-27-7

DEDICATION

I would like to thank my mom and dad. We all did the best we could with the information and tools we had at the time. My dad was my first exposure to philosophy and thinking about the world. He laid the foundation for how I think of things. My mom gave me the feeling side. I had unconditional love from Mom, and I still carry that with me today.

TABLE OF CONTENTS

INTRODUCTION

E ach person brings to this planet a unique combination of all of their experiences and what they have been exposed to. I believe there is universal truth; in fact, I believe your body knows when it hears truth and will give you feedback. I can hear universal truth in many places, whether spiritual or religious, popular culture or not well known, and even obscure sources. My body gives me information if I pay attention and tune in to how it feels in response to information.

- How does your body feel when I talk about love?
- How about when I talk about our current economic picture?
- Does one feel open and expansive?
- Does one feel contractive and heavy?

No opinions or judgment; the information you get from your body is just that, information that you can use to make choices.

I hear many people, especially in the spiritual personal growth realm, saying what I feel is universal truth. I hear similar information from many places. If there is a body of common information or universal truth, what does each person bring? It is my opinion that there is this information available to everyone. Each person is an amazing combination of countless variables to become who they are today.

- What did you read?
- What posts did you run across on social media?
- What really struck your interest and you did more research?

Your individual experiences make up a unique combination that is not replicated by anyone else. That is what I believe each person brings to earth—their unique experiences filtered through their unique personality means each and every one of us has a unique contribution to this existence. We each bring something unlike anyone else. And each one's ultimate expression contributes to the expansion of life. So, every single individual has a totally unique contribution. Honor each individual as they each bring their own gifts.

I heard recently that faith and fear both require you to believe in something you can't see. In other words, there is no hard evidence to confirm your beliefs whether you believe in God or not, whether you believe in an afterlife or not, or whether that shadow in the corner of your room is a robber or not. Shirley MacLaine wrote in her book, *Out on a Limb*, of sitting all night in meditation. When she would open her eyes, she kept seeing a snake in the corner of the room. She never saw it move but was afraid and worried all night long. In the light of day, she finally saw that it was a small length of coiled rope that she had seen. But she spent hours being afraid. How often are we afraid of something that we have no evidence is real or true. I heard an acronym for the word fear from Dr. Wayne Dyer—False Evidence Appearing Real. Fear is usually not based in fact but is a feeling. Faith is also a feeling. Whether your faith is a formally religious form or a spiritual set of beliefs, you use the feeling to determine what you follow. There is no certainty or irrefutable information for the history of religion or using energy medicine. Followers of anything have decided for themselves what resonates as true, and it is from that feeling that they make choices. So, if you have the ability to choose something that you will take action upon based on a feeling of what resonates, it makes sense that where you put your attention, what you focus on is what you are creating.

- So, where is your attention?
- What are you focusing on through faith or fear?
- And can you determine what feels good and expansive and what feels heavy and contractive?
- Can you keep focused on what feels good? That is the simple but not easy task.
- Even in the face of the news and the negativity and everything else that comes at you in a day, can you continue to pay attention to the positive?

There are statistics about everything, but they have measured the overwhelming amount of information and stimulus we are exposed to every day. Our bodies have done a lot of evolving, but it is my opinion that our bodies have not kept up with this exponential growth. Normal growth is when a person walks out their front door and takes 30 steps. They will be about 90' away from their gate, estimating about 3' per step. But exponential growth means the first step is 3', the next is double so 6', then 12', etc. so you can see how much farther you travel. Same with us—take internet access—first there was dial up, then we had ethernet, then Wi-fi that has gone through many increases, and finally 5G speeds. There has been exponential growth in the information access area.

Another common example of exponential growth is the lily pond. Take a pond, free of lilies. For a while, it looks like the growth is slow, just one lily the first day, then two the next day, then four, and so on. If you were swimming around in the pond, for the first three weeks, it would be easy to avoid bumping into a lily. Even after four weeks (28 days), three quarters of the pond is still free of lilies. Plenty of time to act you might think. But the very next day, day 29, the lilies cover half the pond, and your time to act is up. One more day and the lilies have taken over the entire pond. That is the speed of exponential growth, and we are currently experiencing that in so many areas.

Our bodies have changed quite a bit, but I believe we still haven't kept up with the pace of change. I can tell, for myself, that I have a shorter attention span. I don't just sit and daydream as I used to because I reach for something—phone or my laptop. Maybe that is part of the evolution moving forward and maybe it is purely distraction. What ultimately matters to me right here and right now is, does that serve me or bring me down?

That choice is an example of simple not easy. This book is meant as a way to explore many concepts that, on the surface, may seem simple but often in practice are anything but easy. I wrote this book as a tool for thinking about some of these concepts and with the hopes that by doing so, you dear reader, might make some of the steps to make small (or big) impactful changes in your life that will bring you more peace, joy, and even enlightenment.

PART ONE

LEARNING ABOUT WHO WE ARE AND WHAT WE REALLY WANT

CHAPTER 1

LISTENING AND LEARNING FROM YOUR BODY

Our bodies know the truth, always. It's a matter of whether you are honoring and listening to your body or not. For me, I drove my body for years. I just forced her, and forced her, and forced her, and I didn't care what she needed or wanted, because I was not listening. "I'm going to drive you without food until I get so hangry people don't want to be around me. I'm going to drive you with no sleep, and I'll sleep when I'm dead." Now, I dislike that phrase. I'll sleep when I'm dead. Does it feel good to read it? Does it feel good in your body to say it or even think it?

It is not honoring of your body. How do you know what is honoring of your body? If you tune in, does this feel open, expansive, light, warm? That's your body telling you how she feels at this current moment. We override so much, but what if we gave ourselves grace and listened instead?

But if we tune in, our body will tell us what is true for our body. I believe it is individual for every single person to learn what the signals are in their own body. I do believe those signals are unique to each individual. I know what it is for me; it is a sensation in my body. I don't like to give specific descriptions about the sensation because each individual should find it for themselves. Don't take what works for me. Please find it in your own body. It was not long ago when I said, "Honey, do you want to go to work?" And my body was like, "No, I don't want go to work." And I don't think it was this office or this job, but instead my body was just ready to move in a different direction than a Monday through Friday, eight to five sit in my chair job. That's just where I was and I had never asked her that question before. I think we do that a lot. Either we are unconscious and never ask, or we may hear the information but then we override what our bodies are asking for.

One method that has had a big impact on me was from Access Consciousness. One teaching is to stay in the question. Our minds desire answers. The mind is most content when it can say "Oh, that is what this thing is, I can categorize it as a threat or safe." Our minds do not want to stay in the middle of not defining some-thing; it can't be put in a category. It doesn't matter if you answer the question because when you answer things, you lock them in. They become solid and immovable, whereas when you stay in the question, it's wondering, it's possibility, it's open. I realized that I hadn't ever asked my body what an experience was here to teach me and to show me. So, I was in a meeting and that thought came up—*why have I been going through this physical challenge?* We were in a meeting, and I was thought, *That's okay. I will take time and get the answer later,* but we did some somatic movement, and baby girl, my beautiful body, decided to make sure that I heard the an-swer right then. And she said, "Please love me."

Your body has all sorts of ways to keep you safe. For some people, you may hear or get a knowing that is very strong and definitive. Driving is an example; you go to and from work the same way every day. One day you hear in your head "turn here." Or you get some other message like "Don't go to that party" or "Don't turn here." Sometimes it is just that you can't get out of the house on time. I find that often, most times in fact, if you honor the voice or knowing, you will never know what might have happened. What has just been averted? Or was I just meant to explore somewhere I had never been? And maybe that won't be useful until a couple of years from now. Do you need to know? You have choice. Always. Is it enough to just honor the gift of the knowledge and go on gratefully? So many people have stories of big events like 9/11 where they did or did not get on that plane, train, so many things. They are memorable because of the event, but no more or less value and importance than any other guidance you may get. The key is in being calm and peaceful enough to hear information, and then to take action. I believe the honoring is in the action. You can hear information, but if you disregard it, bulldoze over it, don't believe it, then it is not being honored. But if you treat the information as a gift, a sacred knowing then you not only open to that moment but also pave the way smoother for more to come to you in future.

I think we are afraid to trust instinct, and our body is a lot of what instinct is. I grew up in the South. I think that of anywhere I have lived, the South is the most passive aggressive. It meets the exact definition of saying one thing in front of a person and another behind their back. "Bless your heart,"- if you hear that, you know exactly who they are! It has taken so long for me to understand my childhood and growing up in the South. At that time, in the sixties and seventies, what I learned was it didn't matter what I wanted. Maybe I was asked if I wanted to go to a party or to an event or an outing and maybe I said, no I didn't want to go. But given when and where it was, I was told by my parents that my feelings and my wants did not matter. That's because my wishes and wants were overridden, and I was told I had to go do it anyway. For so many reasons, like societal pressure and what's accepted, so much judgment was out of my control. That judgment pointed toward me made me point judgment toward myself. So, for me, that was the beginning of the long history of not honoring my own best interests, wants, or needs. I knew what she wanted, but it didn't matter what I/she wanted as a child. That was going to be overridden. And that started me doubting what I asked for, then doubting myself, then eventually shutting down all the communication. I may have heard the messages, but my mind was driving me forward with total disregard.

We often speak of the mind, body, and spirit or soul. I find it fascinating how many times things come in threes. I remember a freshman English course about Neil Simon. During one section, we discussed the idea that things were funny in threes. We counted those quips and jokes in sets of three in so many of his plays! Back to mind, body, spirit. I think of them as the mind is contained in the brain. The brain is a physical thing that is mostly tasked with keeping us alive. It assesses danger, safety, pain, etc. It handles all our physical systems, conscious or unconscious. Our bodies are just that—a physical embodiment in this lifetime. Our spirit or soul, to me, is our connection to Greater, whatever that looks like to you. I understand atheism, but to me that is not my outlook. I have long felt that there had to be something greater than just this. I believe my soul is a part of Source. That is my word; I am sure you have your own. My soul is the part of me that existed before I came into this body and my soul will continue after my body is no more.

The most important function of the mind is to keep you alive, right? So, maybe it's not going to make the best choices for you or the most expansive choices because its whole purpose is to try to keep you safe. I was talking to the chiropractor, looking for help. I said, "I've been asking my body… Do you want to get on the treadmill? Do you want to get on the rebounder? And she said, No." This is even though I know movement will help me. His answer was, "You have to remember your mind and your body want to keep you from pain. So yes, getting out, moving, being on the treadmill, the rebounder is what you need, but your body's going to say, 'I don't want to hurt, I am trying to keep you from pain.'" So, I try to consider the source of the information I get at any moment and use discernment in taking action.

Recently, I have been having pain and swelling in my fingers and feet. Sometimes it can get overwhelming. I find that when I am in a lot of pain, my mind goes to the possibility of leaving this earthly existence. It seems like a viable choice at times. I spent some time asking questions of my body. Here is my understanding—my mind and body will try and avoid pain. When the pain becomes too much to bear, my mind sees leaving here as a way to not be in pain. When I ask my body, she says she still wants to live. So, now I understand my protection mechanism. My mind and body are doing the absolute best they can. And it is almost always a temporary condition. Even if, at the time, it feels like the only thing on earth, it is not. It will change. And since it is temporary, is it real forever? No. Staying in the question, confirming who I am speaking to and understanding their motivation and where they come from, all this will help to inform this moment and the next and the next.

The pinnacle of Simple Not Easy is that every single moment of every day and every choice can be as simple as is this light/heavy, warm/cool, expansive/contractive, or good for me/not for my highest good. Use the tool of sensations in your body to answer questions. That is Mastery Level. *It is a simple concept but very difficult to stay there 24/7.*

CHAPTER 2

THE HUMAN EXPERIENCE OF EXISTENCE

I remember where I was when I first heard, "You are not a human being having a spiritual experience, you are a spiritual being having a human experience." I found this to be profound and life changing. First, I was no longer afraid of death. How can you die if you are a spiritual being? And this turning around of perspective led me to many other personal beliefs and observations. I do believe we are energetic beings of light and energy, and being here, we have chosen to come in to have this physical experience. There is one point of view out there that we choose to come into this existence; in fact, we choose who we will experience this with and what challenges we want to have. I believe that may be true.

I also have come to view this existence as being in a holodeck, you know like *Star Trek*. We choose to come into human bodies, but we are still spiritual energetic beings. There is also a point of view that as babies, we have not forgotten fully who we are as spiritual beings. In his book, *5 Astounding Recollections of Heaven from Children*, by Dr. Wayne W. Dyer he recounts stories by children about remembering Heaven, choosing parents and siblings, etc. It is a slow process once here to enter this world fully and forget the experience of the other side.

Let's say for the sake of argument that we accept or believe that we are spiritual beings of light and energy. So, in my imagined view, we are just clouds of energy, floating around. Attracted to like energy, repelled by vibration that is not in resonance with us. And then we get an opportunity to go to Earth School and have a body. A meat suit. A sensory input device. That looks really attractive if you have been floating around for a while! What a good gig! Everyone wants in! Who knows, but that is one possibility.

The holodeck idea fits for me because we say, "you create your own reality." What better way to attract what fits with your vibration than immediate or almost immediate drawing in of what resonates with your vibration? We get pulled into this 3D idea of how solid and real and unchangeable this lifetime is. Really? How many people do you see who have changed to the point you observe they are a "new" person? How can two people who had almost the exact same childhood experience with abuse and trauma have different reactions? One can use it as motivation to be different and never go back to that situation again, and another can choose to stay in blaming and victim mode and never move out of the situation. Same experiences, different outcomes, all due to perspective and motivation. Choice is the most magnificent gift we have as humans. You can have made the exact same choice for years and years until one day, you choose differently.

IT'S A MATTER OF CHOICE

One popular artist who has totally impressed me with his choices lately is Jellyroll. I was first aware of him when I saw him at the Grammys a couple of years ago, and since he was a country artist, I didn't really pay much attention. I saw him recently on Jay Shetty's podcast, *On Purpose*. He spoke about his new album *Unbroken* and also the work he has done on himself. I could tell from listening that he has indeed done a lot of personal work. This is a man who grew up in a situation few get out of—poverty, addiction, mental illness in the family. He did not make the best choices as a kid and wound up serving time in jail. However, beating all the odds, he turned things around and got his music career started. The piece of news that made the difference was that while he was incarcerated, he learned he had a child. That was his motivation. You change your behavior because you want to help someone outside of yourself. And he simply made the choice and kept making it. It was not a straight line from there. He was still in and out of jail a couple of times, but if you keep making the choice when you can, you will get there.

I have the utmost respect for anyone who is able to change, stop, or get rid of generational trauma. We have heard that abused children often become abusers, or children of alcoholics become alcoholics themselves. It is all these people have known, so unless they can somehow see themselves as different or have someone to show them another way, they make the same choices as their parents because that is all they know. It sounds simple to just make a choice, but it takes bravery, and courage, and conviction, and it is NOT easy.

To have a choice implies that you have the freedom to make a choice. It can be a place of entitlement, but anyone has this capacity regardless of circumstances. How many unconscious choices do each of us make every day? Driving is a good example. Have you ever come out of your thoughts and don't remember the last stretch of road? But you did drive it, just on autopilot because you weren't present in that moment. Where else have you made choices because of prior experience, well-worn patterns, because that is what is expected, or anything else on the list of reasons we make a choice unconsciously. So, that is the trick, the very first step— recognize it. See where you made a choice without thinking or consideration. You may not change it, but you see it. That should be celebrated to the heavens. You are doing something differently. Congratulate yourself every time you see it. So many don't, so give yourself credit. You are responding when you make a choice, not reacting.

"You can chain me, you can torture me, you can even destroy this body, but you will never imprison my mind".
Mahatma Gandhi

CHOOSING FREEDOM

I was in a group discussion the other night, and we were talking about freedom. The question was posed: What makes you feel free? There were many answers, being in your heart, authenticity, safety, etc. But the one that struck me was choice. Choice is freedom. What does that mean? People who believe they do not have choice are choosing victim mode. The very definition of a victim is that things are happening to them, and they do not have input or control over their own life. This belief or perspective means that everything is external to me. I am subject to the whims of the wind blowing or others are doing something to me. So, you personally have no power or responsibility for what happens to you. If all of life is what happens to you, not what you are choosing and creating, in some ways it is much easier. You can blame external forces, whatever those are. It is similar to seeing things as only black or white, no gray in the middle. That is kind of simple when you can put things in either the black or white box. It certainly satisfies our minds that want to sort things into safety or a threat. That seems to make sense from one point of view. *Look what happened to me, look what they did to me; I am making the best of the situation that I can.*

So, how does that last sentence feel? The victim mentality is, as I said, easier in some ways. You did not cause this, it happened to you, you have no choice, you are just floating, and these events just happen. But how does that feel? Does it feel true? Does it feel empowering? Does it feel better to know you do have choice? I don't believe that victimhood is our true nature. I have a hard time feeling the truth in coming to this physical existence just to float around and react. To react as if we don't have our own power, truth, and agency. That does not feel good in my body. It can be a perfectly valid choice of what you want to experience in human form, in this lifetime. But, choosing my next path, considering options before taking action, finding the action that is for my highest good—those feel good. They feel that I have my own power and agency. The reality is that if you are powerless and controlled by others, you are making the choice to give your power and agency away. Some people have harder circumstances than others. Some are limited and confined in our society. But every single one of us has the source of power within us. Regardless of outside situations, regardless of what is happening to you, you have choice. Maybe you are limited, physically, but no one can take the gift of your mind, your heart, and the limitless part of Source you carry with you—your soul. The gifts are your own thoughts, awareness, and then choice. Even when someone labels you and puts you in a box, you can choose to agree and take on that identity, or you can know that label is not the real, true, authentic you. It is one of the reasons I try to be completely vulnerable and authentic when speaking to others. I can show you all of me, and it does not change who I am. Outside people or forces cannot hurt me; only if I choose to believe what they tell me can they have any influence.

Choice is responding not reacting.

It is easy to do in some situations and harder in others. By responding—not reacting—allows you to find yourself, your truth, your clarity. If you can create that tiny moment of space to see your reaction before taking action and make a considered choice, then you are staying true to yourself. It is so easy to say, but it is difficult to do every day. We also call this mindfulness, which I guess is as good a label as any. It simply means you are paying attention. You place your attention on your emotions, the feelings your body is communicating, and all of what is going on internally, before a knee-jerk reaction. It can start as the smallest, briefest moment. With time and attention, the space can become larger, longer.

To me, the magic is in the moment you recognize either that you are reacting or that you see that space, that moment before you react. We have had so many years of training in our old pathways that even just noticing the smallest moment, the smallest space before the next reaction or thought, is a momentous event. Celebrate yourself if you see it! There should be balloons and confetti and streamers around you! They can be energetic, but it should be celebrated. It should feel good in your body. You will not be perfect; you will see them again and you will miss them again! Perfect, you are human!

From choice and choosing us and our internal responses instead of unconscious reactions, we are then in our own truth and power. We listen and are influenced by the messages and information within us. Whether that is tuning in to how our body feels about something or tuning into our soul messages, we are guiding ourselves in our own truth. Even if it doesn't make sense to anyone else.

I love synchronicities, and while writing this, I just looked at an email from Liz Gilbert's Substack and she cited an article which said it has been studied that it is kinder to speak to yourself in the second person than in the first person. She used the example of "I am overwhelmed." That is first person, and you are now that identity. It is who you see yourself as. It may or may not be true, but you are now living that label. Instead, you could say "You are overwhelmed, sweetheart." Now, overwhelm is not who you are, but something you are going through. It is an experience, not an identity. And an experience is way more flexible than an identity. Once you have said, "I am . . ." you have limited yourself, closed yourself off from possibilities. So, which feels better and more empowering? I will go with that little bit of space from "I am" to "I see you are." And in that space, you now have choice to stay the same or make a change. Make another choice.

CHOICE AND CONTROL

Here is an illustration of control and how I resolved my area of control for myself. When I lived in New York, in Brooklyn, recycling was mandatory. They would kick your bags of trash, and if they heard cans or bottles, they would give the building a fine. I examined why I recycled, because there were so many people who didn't. Why did I keep making the choice if it was available to me to go to the extra effort of recycling? Why do I keep recycling when statistics show most does not get recycled? I decided for myself that I was only in charge of my choices and the choice to recycle felt better than the choice to just throw it in the trash. I can only make choices for myself. I have no control over other's choices; I just have to be true to me and what is important to me.

I have talked about where you have control and where you don't. It is a pretty narrow band of just yourself. That is all you actually have control of. You can try to control other people, events, or things, but that is rarely successful and often fills you with frustration and lack of control and anxiety and burdens that you carry. But, remember how powerful you are within your sphere of control. You can create anything—*anything*. But anything encompasses, well, anything and everything! You can create muck just as well as light and growth. I can examine my own life and see that I have created both what I wanted and what I didn't. It is not an easy place to take responsibility or be accountable for what has happened to you. It seems terrible sometimes to say, "I created that" or "I manifested that" when it is not a pleasant experience.

I don't think you can come here to this life of being human, and they are all going to be pleasant experiences. But, you can ask more empowering questions once you have taken responsibility for your choices and manifestation. An event occurs that is maybe traumatic or dramatic or in some way disturbs your peaceful life.

In the past, you might have gone into victim mode and said, "Why did X make this happen? Why me? I don't deserve this." But if you look at all of life as serving you, as the physical representation of your energy and vibration, and ask, "What is this here to show me? Why did I call this into my life?"

For me, that is a much more empowering place to be. And the questions I ask give me more clarity and information to stay in a frequency or vibration that creates the results I am looking for. It is all just choice. It is all just choosing that which is expansive, not contractive. I saw a Mel Robbins quote that you are one decision away from a new life. One choice, one decision, one new vibration and your whole life can change. Simple not easy. I know the vibration that feels good and is productive for me, but I do not stay there 24/7. I do my best knowing the target and trying to spend as much time there as I can. And when I fall short, I give myself grace. I choose not to beat myself up for the times I didn't stay in the best vibration. It is in the past and can't undo that, but I make the best choice I can going forward. Forward, expansion, love, and grace.

You are amazing. See your own light. Stand in your own light and power. And then be seen. You don't really have to do, just be. Stand in your power and shine and be seen. That can be scary, but when you come from your own power and your own truth, you will show your authenticity and that is powerful. And further, when you are standing in your own light and power, can any outside force actually cause you harm? Maybe on a material basis, but no one can touch who you are, your values and ethics, and your authentic power. Doesn't that feel good? Don't you feel strong? But it is a quiet personal power, not an outward show of power. As Dr. Wayne Dyer said, "When you change the way you look at things, the things you look at change." You did not change these outside events that "happened" to you, but you changed the way you look at them. You were not a victim of what happened to you, but you are able to gather information about why you brought this to yourself and what you are being shown or what you can learn to grow and change the next time.

CHAPTER 3

MY STORY AND HOW I GOT HERE

I'm going to tell my story. It will be linear but with commentary that has been gained over the years and took a while to get to!

I don't believe I have a lot of very early childhood memories. Maybe some flashes, but it's a little hard for me to tell if I actually remember them or if they're from family stories and family pictures.

FIRST MY PARENTS...

My dad was English and about 16 years older than my mother. He came with all of the stoicism and stiff upper-lipness that you would expect from someone who was born during World War I and lived through World War II while helping to support his parents. He was quite an interesting man, a philosopher, by trade mechanical engineer, and a cyclist. He had polio when he was about 18 months old, and I believe that affected a lot in his life. He always worked hard to not walk with a limp and hide his disability. In fact, he tried to enlist in the English army in World War II, but between his extreme nearsightedness and his one disabled leg, he was not able to. He did tell stories about how persistent he was. First, he went in with his glasses and immediately it was no. Then he went in without his glasses, and he couldn't see well enough to fill out the form so that was also no. I know where I get my stubbornness from, actually both parents!

My dad was a draftsman for Vickers Armstrong airplane factory during the war in England and one of his jobs was to travel the countryside and try to find spaces where they could have satellite factories. They would make parts of the plane in different places and only bring it all together at the end and get that plane into the air. So, if one satellite factory was hit, they didn't lose the whole plane. Because he was a cyclist, he would travel great distances on his bicycle searching the countryside. He also relayed to me how grateful he was to live in the US, after experiencing a dark country road on his bicycle and seeing German planes flying overhead. He wound up moving to Canada and working for a hydroelectric plant in Toronto after the war. England was completely depleted, and he sent back money, food, anything he could to help out with the family. His mom and dad were old age pensioners by this time meaning retired and they lived with his sister, brother-in-law, and two daughters. Dad went back to England as a young man, searching for what he was going to do next. He told me that as soon as he stepped off the plane in England, he knew it had not been the right decision. But he stayed, and he had his best cycling season with his local club—the Mersey Roads Cycling Club. I still have his plaque that commemorates that season in 1951.

Later, as a family, they decided to move to Toronto, Canada. As soon as they were back in Canada, and my dad was working and saving money, he had his eye on coming into the US, stopping for a while, working, saving more money, exploring the country, and then exploring the world. He thought he was on his way to a final destination of New Zealand. Short story, he made Richmond, Virginia, his first stop as New York was too big and he didn't like it . He didn't like Philadelphia either, and then he met my mother in Richmond and he never went any farther on his world tour.

My mother was the oldest of six kids in a Catholic German family in Richmond. Those were some tough times. There were the three oldest children, then a long gap where there were miscarriages, stories of a baby girl buried in a cigar box, a little boy who lived to about twoyears old and then passed away and then the three youngest. It was a large age gap between the oldest and the baby, and when my mother took my aunt, the youngest out, people often thought it was her child.

I believe that my mom was a dutiful, obedient child even though she also had a spicy, fiery, funny personality, and she used to joke with her siblings. I remember them telling stories about childhood trips in the station wagon with a ton of kids and the fun they used to have. My mom went to college and took a job as a social worker in Baltimore after school. Funny story actually, my mother started college to be a teacher in the mid-50s since there were not too many paths open. At that time, you didn't do your classroom experience until the end of your last semester. Once she actually experienced the classroom, my mother realized she did not like teaching, so she went into social work. I believe she was living her best young life in Baltimore, but then my grandfather became ill, and she came home to help the family. They ran a small store, and there were still young kids at home, so she went to help.

My parents met in the theater. I am not actually sure what led my dad into acting, but he was good from what I read, hear, and remember. My mother performed in plays and musicals in college and possibly high school. Dad was new in Richmond and found that the Hanover Tavern needed help as Barksdale Theater was just beginning. I am not certain how Mom got involved, but the often-cited family story was they built an outdoor Amphitheater in Virginia in the summer amid humidity and mosquitoes! The show they were doing was an original about the history of Virginia and the title of it was *To Rise One Day!* They all fondly called it, *To Flop One Night.* But that was where my parents met. My mother saw my

31

dad putting on his makeup and said, "That's the man I'm going to marry," and she did.

So, theater was around me from before I was born. My mom actually went to a dress rehearsal of *Once Upon a Mattress* on Friday night when she was pregnant and about to have me. The story goes that she went into labor about midnight, they finally went to the hospital about noon the next day, and I was born at 5:00 p.m. on the dot. One of my strongest childhood memories is when my father performed at Barksdale Theater in *The Fantastiks*. That should have been the time when I figured out I was gay because I was head over heels for the young woman who played the girl. She was very kind to me and on closing night gave me her plastic beads and plastic flower that she had worn in the show. I was over the moon and kept them for many, many years. But that story didn't enter my awareness until much later.

My dad was involved in a car accident when I was little, maybe five or so. He was driving his VW bus to work one winter morning when several cars hit a patch of ice. The bus rolled but somehow landed on its wheels. Dad was wearing a seat belt, but the compression of coming down fractured a couple of his vertebrae. I remember him wearing a full body cast for a while, then a brace that supported his entire torso. Several years later, the damage caused some bone spurs and scar tissue that caused him trouble for the rest of his life. When I was in junior high, I think, Dad had trouble with back spasms caused by the damage in his back. I remember one night where he was flat on the living room floor and the spasms were so bad, he could not move, much less get up off the floor. The rescue squad took him to the hospital. I was hanging around watching all of this, and it made a huge impression on me. It was the first time I had seen my dad incapacitated; the first time he was not the strong, infallible, capable man I knew. It shook me to see him on the floor. But I could only deal with that on my own. I never spoke about it with either Mom or Dad. My go-to place was to hold it inside, don't share, don't talk, and ruminate on my own.

And usually, whatever I was rolling around in my head was not true, or not totally true, and I had no help to process it and reach a healthy conclusion.

MORE FAMILY HISTORY

Dad talked about his sister especially, but also his mom. In his opinion, they were not mentally healthy or solid. His sister cut off communication with people in her own family for years, including one of her daughters. She did not like the man my cousin chose to marry so she decided she would not attend the wedding, and because she was in control, she forbade her husband to attend as well. My cousin's wedding was the reason for my first trip to England with my family. My dad gave his niece away at her wedding. Eventually, when my cousin and her husband had a child, the grandchild created a thaw, and the family was connected again. My dad's sister still carried resentment over Dad giving away his niece at the wedding, and she cut off contact for many years. It was only in the last few years of both my dad and his sister's life that they reconciled. That was after both of their spouses had passed away. Actually, my cousin set up a surprise meeting between my dad and his sister when we were there visiting. It was wonderful to see them reunite, and all the years of silence and resentments fall away. It was so easy once everyone set their stuff down. It can be incredibly simple to reconnect. It does require that both people are ready to leave the past behind, let go of your old stuff—usually on both sides—and open your heart.

Given this history and what my dad was shown and learned from his family experience, it is not surprising that he basically did the same thing to my mom. He may not have left, gotten divorced, and split up the family, but that may have been better. Since he was angry with my mom but felt trapped in the marriage, he left in another way. He was just unavailable emotionally. He essentially did leave, at least in connection with Mom and me. He would go into his den where he would write behind closed doors for hours. I walked on eggshells with him, so he did not get mad over whatever. All this is only evident in hindsight. At the time, this was all I knew so I thought this was normal. I thought every family was like this. It is only after seeing other families and how it could have been different that I realized my upbringing was not healthy, nor did it give me good tools and coping mechanisms.

It must have been the same vibration between my parents of what they had been shown about staying connected with family, that also meant my mom's mother did the same thing to my mom. She didn't like my mom's choice of my dad as a husband. So, my mom's parents did not attend their wedding. It was my mom's aunt and her husband that hosted my parents' reception after their wedding at city hall. Again, the grandchild created a change. My grandmother eventually came around to be open for contact again. My mom and her mom were very close in all of my memories. And my mom and Grandma would go and do all sorts of things. I think it was of interest to them, but it also took Mom out of the house and away from my dad's negative energy. When I was old enough, I did it all with them—house tours, garden tours, railroad trips, the Daffodil Mart, the Pork Festival, and yearly events that they enjoyed. It gave me a lot of time with the two of them, memories that I treasure. But I think it also showed me that marriage is not two people pulling together, but two people cohabiting and just trying to keep the anger contained. Whew!

I grew up as an only child, and we lived in a rural area where there was a 500-acre Farm across the road and a 500-acre Farm to the north. The few of us kids in the neighborhood could roam across the land all day and still be on someone's property who knew us. I believe things were "normal" with my parents up until the time I was about five. My mother was 29 when I was born and my dad was 45. Mom would come and go out of jobs, so I'm not sure if she was working at that time or not. My father suspected that my mother was taking cash out of his wallet, and the first time he confronted her, she denied it. So, he set her up so she could not deny it and from that moment until about a week before she passed away my father became distant, isolated, emotionally unavailable, and angry. His words to me were, "Well, this is my lot in life, and I'll just have to do the best I can." So, there was a massive undercurrent of anger between my parents. As a child, I didn't know what was wrong, and it wasn't talked about or explained to me; so, I took it on as my fault. If there was trouble between my parents, I was the only other one there, so it must be my fault. I know this is really common for children to take this on but how unfair. As life went on, there would be stony silence, not talking until it couldn't be contained, and it bubbled over into a yelling screaming match. Observing my parents also never taught me how to fight because I thought after watching them that in the heat of anger you could say anything and no one ever left. That was only true between my parents, and it ill-prepared me for arguments and conflict with anyone else.

My father's child-rearing philosophy was that I was to be treated just as a small adult. I was smart, I could understand things, and he would just speak to me as a small adult. It would not serve me well. Sometime when I was maybe 10 or 12, when my father expressed grave concern over the fact that I was angry and showing anger, he made me a bag with I don't even know what in it and a couple of sticks so that I could just beat it and work out my anger. He told me that he was very concerned because I was showing signs of mental illness like his mother and his sister. What was I going to do with that? Stuff it, stuff it, stuff it, never talk about it, and the only safe place for me to put any anger was inside me directed at myself. I must be wrong. I must be bad. I must be stupid. I don't do anything right, and when I'm angry, I will just direct it inward and beat the ever-loving crap out of myself.

When I was about 13 or 14, my mom's health took a turn. She was diagnosed with psoriasis and psoriatic arthritis. She was hypertensive, and at one point diabetic. They sat me down and told me how things were going to be. Dad and I were to take on all of the household chores. I was to have dinner ready and on the table when they arrived home about 5:30. Even if I had used my voice, now it was not okay to use my voice; everything was focused on my mother and her health. There was no room for me to say what I wanted or I needed. I probably wouldn't have asked anyway as I had already developed a well-worn pattern of not talking. Oddly, I remember that this was also exactly the time when I began cursing at my parents. F-bombs and everything. As I look back now, it was fueled by all this anger and lack of self-worth and my parents didn't come down hard on me. I'm not sure why. Maybe they thought it was a phase that would blow over or... *we're going to get her out of the house to go to college in a few years so we'll just put up with it.* I have no idea. I don't think anyone in that house was really happy.

CHAPTER 4:

STARTING REAL LIFE

E ventually, I graduated from high school and indeed went to college in Charlotte, North Carolina, to a small all-girls college at the time called Queens College. I went as a bio-chemistry major and that was really to please my dad. I had been doing theater since junior high school and had caught the light-ing-design bug. I loved doing lighting. It is interesting to me that I have met so many, especially tech theater people, who also have a connection to science and biology in particular. I am not sure where that parallel comes from.

My freshman year was the first time I was away from home and able to make my own choices. I made some very interesting ones, like I thought it was so much easier to sleep in my sleeping bag and not have to make up my bed. I also discovered drinking for the first time, especially being able to do that on a regular basis. It was a pattern that lasted for a very long time thinking... *I may not drink every single day, but if I do start drinking I'm not going to stop until I am unconscious.* It took me a very long time to learn the lesson of being able to just have one or two drinks and not get stupid and to actually enjoy it. It was numbing. I was taking myself to the point of obliteration, so I didn't have to be aware and then my sophomore year, I was finally awakened to my sexuality as a lesbian.

By the end of that year, I had moved in with my ex-security guard girlfriend who got fired because we were together. I still have shame about the fact that I thought about (and we discussed at the time) bringing a lawsuit. In the early '80s, I'm not sure how far that lawsuit might have gotten in Charlotte, NC, but I knew that I did not want the spotlight on me or to live through what I could see that lawsuit would mean in my day-to-day life. It was about that time that I also learned one of my greatest lessons, which was to live life without regrets. I will say that I don't have many. It may be that choice is one that I still think about, but I'm not sure if it's with regret or recognition of that past choice.

That first relationship with the security guard taught me so much as I had never dated; in fact, that would continue for a long time, perhaps to the present day. I did not feel worthy, so if someone paid the least bit of attention to me, I would grab onto it like a drowning person to a life jacket. There was no discernment or evaluation of values, commonalities, or compatibility. I felt that if this person was attracted to me, then I should take it because it was the last time I might get the opportunity that someone would find me attractive. It was at that time during fights while in a relationship with a 29-year-old woman who got fired and her 19-year-old girlfriend, that bitterness and resentment built. During those fights, I learned that, unlike my parents, you can't just say anything in the heat of a fight and then no one leaves. That is what I had observed in my parent's marriage but came to find out that didn't apply to everyone's relationships. It was an important lesson to learn. Say what you mean and no idle threats or threats you are not ready to follow through with.

It took some time to remember and understand a moment I had with my first lover. In the middle of a fight, I grabbed a textbook and literally started beating myself with it. I smacked myself hard enough that I creased the cover. It was only much later looking back that I realized I was doing that because I literally felt like the only safe place to put anger was at myself. I was berating myself in the middle of that, hitting myself, and calling myself stupid. Let's be clear, one of the last things I am is stupid. I have always been intellectually smart; for Pete's sake during junior high school and maybe into high school, I would go take tests on the weekend for fun. I hope now that I have learned emotional intelligence, which certainly wasn't present in my growing up or in the time that my parents were alive. But that voice that comes to me, which has been around from an early age that tells me I am not worthy, still exists. The best I can do is to know that I have many tools I have found over the years, and with awareness and listening, I can catch that voice or slide toward that pathway faster and make a different choice. It sounds simple to just notice when you are being unkind to yourself but not always easy to be 100% consistent.

My first lover broke up with me sometime shortly after I finished school. She came home and announced to me that she had been having an affair and that the new girlfriend was going to be moving in and that I was going to be moving out. I did no work toward healing after that relationship. I don't think I knew to even consider that then. I had a few drunken one-night stands, and then, for whatever reason, got together with the woman I will always refer to as the straight girl. We were doing *Oliver* in a Holiday Inn banquet room dinner theater, and I thought her voice was awesome and so the attraction between us happened. I know that I have some of the rescuer tendencies and that certainly was present at the start of our relationship. I remember my mom saying at one point that she thought I was way too good for this woman because after we had broken up, I helped move her into her new place and hung a ceiling fan. I did it because of the guilt, shame, not being worthy, and was trying to do something to make up for us having broken up. The reason why it ended was because I was going to grad school back at the University of Virginia, near my childhood home. I had applied to grad schools and at the time, Yale was the premier theater program. The program at Yale intimidated me, so I wound up going where I could get in state tuition.

The same things applied for relationships during grad school. I wound up dating two or three young women for whom I was their first female lover. I am not sure why I made those choices because they, of course, came with a lot of drama and it was quite bumpy. Maybe it fit my rescuer personality or maybe it was a power trip for me, but I was repeating the same patterns. I was being needy and not having a good foundation, much less for a relationship as myself, day to day. It was during this time that my mom had really started to go downhill. During my first year, she had a bad infection and they sent her home over the holidays. I was back from school, and as soon as I arrived, Dad retreated to his room, his den, and left me to care for my mom until I went back to school. It was probably fair enough because he was the caregiver all the rest of the time, but it would have been nice to be clear on his expectations as we never spoke about it. By my last semester, Mom had a stroke in April of that year. I never walked the lawn at the University of Virginia to pick up my diploma, and I think that disappointed Mom a lot. I'm sure she would have loved to see me do that. But I had a job, and I went off to do a gig instead of attending graduation.

One of the best things that happened in grad school was at the beginning of my third (last) year. My lighting design professor had left for another job. For the first semester, I had an alumna who was a professional LD teach, and the second semester, I had another professional. That led to me applying for the Internship for Lighting Designer's Union USA Local 829. After the application process, some were selected for the portfolio review. There were something like three or four Broadway lighting designers there. I don't even remember who anymore, but one of them said, "You know, this is really hard. You should go home, moving to doing this, this internship, it's really hard. You should just go home." I realized later, they probably said that to everybody, and if you believed it, then they were absolutely right, because it is hard. And if you're not up for hard, then you should go home. Don't take somebody else's spot, right? Well, that sentence pissed me off!

When I was accepted, I moved, and I figured I was one of the pack, out looking for work. I had the whole membership list, so it being 1990, pre-emailing, I got a letter printed and copies made. I signed each one, hand wrote out the addresses, stamped the envelopes, and sent those off looking for my first professional gig in NYC. I wrote it like a memorandum.

To: rich, successful lighting designer
From: starving intern
Re: Looking for work

I got the full gamut of replies. One well-known Broadway designer and educator who wrote back and said essentially, "This is insulting. I will never hire you, blah, blah, blah," and I also got my first job out of it. I was hired as an assistant to go to Cleveland and do a show that was supposed to be Broadway-Bound. I'm not sure why it never made it, but it was called *Heart's Desire*. We did it at the Cleveland Playhouse, and I was her assistant. It was my first job working at that level!

CHAPTER 5:

DEALING WITH GRIEF

My mom passed away early on the morning of December 7, 1990. I took the train from NYC to Richmond, VA, and was met by my dad. My memory is a little fuzzy, but I think we even went by the funeral home for some arrangements before going home. I was in what I call deep grief, my state from what I had been shown by other people, movies, etc. I stared a lot and was in my head missing some things.

I think we have gotten worse in this country about handling grief, and most of it is tied to loss of community. Before it became the funeral industry, you often passed away at home and then there was a social protocol. People came to pay their respects, often with food, but they showed up. Certain religious faiths have a defined sequence of events around what happens after death and up to a year after. I think that kind of structure, although it can be rigid and inflexible, can also give a form and structure to one of the worst unstructured, unmoored times in life. Now, we have lost communal grieving and that shared experience, which was talked about and processed together. Francis Weller calls our modern society grief phobic. We may go to the funeral but avoid talking to anyone. We never talk about the one who is no longer here. The most common phrase is "I don't know what to say." No one ever knows what to say because there isn't anything to say that will

43

change or fix the situation. Just showing up and just saying it really sucks and "I love you," is enough.

It is surprising to me that now we have to pick up from podcasts and websites things that we can do to connect with and help other people. I have heard suggestions about what to bring, what to do, and what to say. They are actually excellent suggestions like don't ask the person, "What do you need?" Just show up and do their laundry or some other concrete task that they don't have to make a decision about. I think these suggestions are really helpful to start, but underneath that we have lost empathy and the ability to see what might help someone else without being told or having someone else define what we need to do. Aren't we all intuitive and perceptive people who could look at a situation of loss and come up with something that would be helpful for them? A mother with young children might really appreciate you taking care of the kids for a couple of hours, so she has time for herself. It could be any number of things, but can't we do that on our own? Has the loss of community also meant the loss of empathy and the simple knowledge of how to help someone else? We all have unique talents and gifts. Maybe you can't cook the most delicious casserole, but you can mow and clean up the yard or the pool, or do the laundry, or just sit with them for an hour without talking, listening to music, and being together.

It reminds me of the fact that we don't like to be alone with ourselves in silence. Maybe that is the fear or the ridicule of meditation. You must be comfortable sitting with yourself in silence without distractions to get to many of the other places that are always available to you. Places such as reducing anxiety, feeling love, being in your heart space, and helping your physical body. I grew up as an only child, and I don't think I had my first radio until I was maybe 10 years old and that was followed by a cassette recorder. I spent a lot of my life in silence. There was a time when if I moved, the stereo would be the first thing to get set up. Now when I move, the bed is the first thing that gets set up! I live in silence quite a bit—driving, at home—so it is common for me to spend much of my time in silence. I know this is not common, especially now. We have devices that give us audio distractions 24/7. It used to be that when you went hiking, you heard people walking and talking. Now it is quite common that they are either silent with their headphones on or you hear their speaker. Let's call this what it is—a means of not being present. It is a distraction; it is programming. It removes us from the moment and from our bodies. I need this reminder just as much as anyone else on a daily basis. It is easy for me not to inhabit my body, but I do try and I look for ways that will help me remember to be in my body and to be present.

So, when my mom passed, I grieved the only way I knew how. All I saw was the loss. There were a few really impactful moments during that time. I started my longest relationship while I was still in that deep grief. The dynamic that brought us together was she was the parent, the authoritative figure, and I was the child, the one who did what they were told. It actually functions as a workable relationship dynamic until someone doesn't want to play anymore. After midnight, a few years after my mom passed away, and I was together with my ex, she reminded me that the day before had been December 7th, the anniversary of my mother's death. I was devastated that I did not remember on my own and also let her know that I was very disappointed that she didn't tell me. I would rather have been reminded and honored that day than to wait until it was over and then have her tell me. I also remember a time, maybe five or six months after Mom passed away, and I had gotten so far as to have the phone in my hand to dial her before I remembered she had passed away. That reflexive, knee-jerk reaction to call and tell her something had happened before I could remember she wasn't here. It was like a fresh loss all over again. I have come to be of the opinion that you must be extra kind and give yourself extra grace for the first year after an intense loss. I think every new date, anniversary, and birthday is just the first time you have experienced it without that person. After more years without my mother than I had with my mother, I will say that the journey continues. It is for the most part less intense, but it is certainly one of those spiral vortexes where I come around again to something I have visited before. But I am in a different place, so the experiences are healing or addressing a different part. I think that with forgiveness, when something major first happens and you can reach forgiveness, it might be on a more top or superficial level. And on subsequent visits to that issue, I think you heal deeper and deeper with more compassion, empathy, and forgiveness.

So much in our lives could change or could be held from a different perspective if we could turn things around and see where the other person is coming from. It does require imagination and putting aside our own personal stuff. I try to see that, for example, when driving in traffic. What happened that can make a person drive badly and make choices like a jerk? Did they just have a fight with their partner that day, or a fight with their boss? Did they just lose their job or was it something not so major but still very upsetting? Imagining what someone else may be going through is just the beginning of empathy.

My dad passed away in May of 1997. Princess Diana died in August of that year. It took me a long time to understand why I took her death almost personally. It was a global mourning of her, especially the sudden end to her life. I was as upset as if she were in my own family. Quite some time later, I realized that the loss of Diana was getting tied up with all of the other losses in my life and sort of ping ponging off each other. I had not fully grieved or resolved my mom and my dad and Princess Diana kind of ended up in the same mix. It's weird in retrospect but absolutely real to me at the time. Almost exactly a year later, the last member of my immediate family, my mom's mom passed away. Again, it resonated with all the other losses and plunged me into deep grief. It really took a while to heal, and eventually I was ready to move forward. Looking back now, I could not know that I was ready for a spiritual awakening. But, that is what came to pass. I blew up my longest relationship by having an affair. It was a terrible and most unkind choice. I was unhappy in the relationship. As I said before in a parent/child dynamic, it works great until it doesn't. I was moving out of deep grief and ready for more growth. In fact, as I looked back, I felt like I had not made any progress in growing for a while. This may or may not be accurate, but I was no longer happy in the relationship. The turning point came in the fall of 2000 when I felt a complete betrayal by my partner. From day one I had been clear that I wanted to have a baby. I had a lot of loss, the biological clock was ticking loudly, and I wanted to further my lineage. The Bone name in my branch of the family tree ends with me. My dad had a brother who was killed in WWII, but he only had one daughter. There are more people in the lineage but the name will stop. When we first got together, we lived in NYC and were starving artists, hand to mouth. Eventually, we moved to DC and when my dad had passed away, I inherited the house I grew up in. Both of us were working and we now owned a home together. All the obstacles to having a baby were finally removed. I had been researching and pushing for this to happen. After all, at that point, I had been clear for eight years about what my goal was. When my partner was backed into a corner, she finally said one day that she did not want to have a baby with me. She said she did not want to "raise two kids." I guess from her perspective and our relationship dynamic, that made sense. However, for me, it was the greatest betrayal. I had talked about it from the beginning, and she had eight years to address this mismatch between us.

It was such an impactful moment for me that I still remember where I was standing, time of day, everything about that moment. There was a voice in my head that said *leave right now.* I didn't, and then I got mad. I said, "Well, then I am spending my money" and I bought a bicycle and got back into shape. I used the bike as a way to be out of the house for long periods of time. That anger fueled me into having the affair. As I said, it was incredibly effective at ending the relationship but the most unkind choice I could make. The issue was our lack of communication, and my anger at what I saw as a betrayal. But, the affair made it become about the "other woman." I did stay with that other woman for several years, but based on my unhealed state and issues, I created another unhappy relationship.

I moved with the other woman to Florida, and she started an animal rescue out of the house. She was supposed to bring in money to support the rescue, but as I later found out, she had been taking money out of my savings and did not tell me about it. Another major betrayal that I created. Another relationship based on anger and terrible communication. And I also spent silly long hours on the bike doing ultra long-distance bike races. And again, looking back, I used that to beat myself up. Long hours in the saddle, soreness, numbness, just tearing myself down. Because if I was angry, it was still (I was in my 40s at this point) the only safe place for my anger was directed at myself. Directing it at others was not a good idea, although when the anger would boil over, I did direct it outward.

One of the things that came out of the relationship with the other woman was my spiritual awakening. She found out about The Secret and that was the beginning. We went to events and seminars, and my world started to open up. It was one of the greatest shared experiences I have had. We still share a friendship and a bond born out of that spiritual awakening.

MORE ABOUT GRIEF

I have had a lot of experiences with grief. My first and deepest experience was when my mother passed away when I was 28. My mother's father had passed when I was five and my father's mother had passed when I was in my teens, but none had the impact that losing my mother had. It was my first real loss and I hadn't been shown very many good tools to get through it, so I went into deep grief, which is what I thought I was supposed to do. Honestly, it was the only thing I knew how to do.

More recently, I have come to see many of the other ways the grief manifests. There is not any one of us who didn't have at least one thing, if not many things, to grieve during the pandemic. Whether it was the loss of a person, a family member, a friend, loved one, or the loss of a job or the loss of going to the office, or any of the myriad losses we all went through. I would offer that if you think you didn't have any or you think that it wasn't that big a deal, I would suggest that it maybe something for you to look at.

Even more recently, I lost my job in Las Vegas. I actually manifested losing that job because I was deeply unhappy at the company; however, when you are called into the meeting with HR and let go, it is still shock and the loss is still grief. As always, the universe took care of me and I had a job offer two days later and took the job in Phoenix. I still had a house, three dogs, and a roommate in Las Vegas so I drove home from Phoenix to Vegas every weekend for three months. Eventually, I was able to get the sale of the house in Vegas and the purchase of the house down here to line up, and I moved in mid-February. All that driving back and forth, the loss of a job, the starting of a new job, the change, that was all loss and grief. I did have extra thrown in as one of my puppy dogs, who I had had a bonus year with because he was in the last stages of kidney disease, let me know that he didn't want to make the trip to Phoenix. He was done, and I let him go the day before the movers came. Six weeks later, here in Phoenix, as a surprise, I did not know how much pain and physical discomfort my 14-year-old dog had been in, but I let her go as well. It took months and I am still working on allowing and releasing all the change and the grief from those months. Give yourself Grace as you do the best you can.

CHAPTER 6

THE MANY PATHS TO HEALING

THE STAR THROWER: A PARABLE

A young girl was walking along a beach upon where thousands of starfish had been washed up during a terrible storm. When she came to each starfish, she would pick it up, and throw it back into the ocean. People watched her with amusement.

She had been doing this for some time when a man approached her and said, "Little girl, why are you doing this? Look at this beach! You can't save all these starfish. You can't begin to make a difference!"

The girl seemed crushed, suddenly deflated. But after a few moments, she bent down, picked up another starfish, and hurled it as far as she could into the ocean. Then she looked up at the man and replied,

"Well, I made a difference for that one!"

The old man looked at the girl inquisitively and thought about what she had done. Inspired, he joined the little girl in throwing starfish back into the sea. Soon others joined, and all the starfish were saved.

I have loved this story for many years. I first heard it around animal rescue. All of my dogs have been rescued, and I have made a difference in their lives. Even if everyone did not join in, each starfish thrown back had a difference made in its life. What if noticing and allowing one small thing in your life is the same thing? You made a huge difference with that one thing in your life. Honor yourself and acknowledge, appreciate, look for those thoughts, moments, or events that you changed or did differently than you did in the past.

I wonder if I have been thinking of healing all wrong. Everything I have always thought about healing talks is that you can let go and it just disappears. I looked up what is healing and this is what came up first:

The true meaning of healing encompasses more than just the absence of illness or injury; it's a process of becoming whole, encompassing physical, emotional, mental, and spiritual well-being, and finding meaning and purpose in the face of adversity.

Becoming whole. I thought that was getting rid of trauma and the shadow side. I thought when I was healed, the un-whole or injured parts would not be there. What if I have been thinking about this all wrong? What if healing is about letting go, but letting go of attachment to that shadow side, letting go of the resistance or avoidance or denial of the Shadow side, of whatever it is that we want to heal? What if healing is welcoming and loving and wholly accepting all the parts? So, after I am healing, those parts are still there. It's not like they go away or disappear. That's not what I'm Letting Go of. Those parts are there and may always be there and I am grateful. Everything that they are came from or represent is part of the journey that brought me here, and I am learning and growing and becoming whole. I think I thought I was trying to eradicate those parts. I think I thought that's what healing is. So, what if those parts will always be with me? What if those parts are part of who I am and my true essence? And what if I loved them? What if I honored them and was grateful for them as much as every other part?

SYNCHRONICITIES

I loved Florida—the weather and temperature suited me. I was active with my bike riding, and it was a mecca. I also am not great at climbing hills and Florida was pretty flat and worked well for me. Work was a roller coaster there. I transferred to the Orlando office from DC, and four months later they let me go. The first time! I found another job with a company in the same business. That went for two years, and then I knew they were looking to let me go, and I was in talks with my old company. It worked out that they did let me go, and the same day, my old company made an offer to bring me back.

I have had several instances in my life with synchronicity to the point where sometimes it is not possible to believe! I think the first time was when my long-term ex and I were looking for a house in the DC Northern Virginia area. My partner was nervous about committing to a 30-year mortgage coming from our starving-artist background. I had a full-time job and was doing well and so we went ahead, did the house hunting, and put in an offer for one place. On the exact same day that we submitted the offer, my ex was offered a full-time job in theater as a stage manager, doing what she was really good at. It was amazing timing.

Another instance was that day when I knew my company was going to let me go, and I had been in talks with my old company. The new company called me first thing in the morning and said after I got back from my vacation that I would no longer be employed with them. I called my current partner, The Other Woman, and asked her to come for lunch. I planned on giving her the bad news there. Between the time when I called her and she got there, my old company called with an offer and we agreed on the day that I would be back after my vacation. Just seamlessly, the universe was taking care of me. My biggest task was to just stay out of the way.

Eventually, the relationship ended with the other woman. It wasn't surprising based on the foundation we started the relationship with, and that I had not done my work and dealt with my issues. I moved out of our house and on my own. Out of my long-distance cycling, one of the things I got interested in was the Race Across America. It is a cross-country bicycle race that has been going for over 40 years. At the time, it went from Oceanside, CA, to Annapolis, MD, though the route has changed a few times over the years. I had friends doing the race, so I volunteered to be on the crew. I wound up doing the full race three times, doing the first part that ended in Boulder, CO twice, and assisting on a couple of other race starts. I found out that I am good at it. The confluence of my organization skills, my ability to stay up for long periods of time, and my ability to both see the big picture as well as be detail-oriented were all put to use on those trips.

Being a white woman in her early sixties makes me privileged in certain ways. I was born in Virginia in 1962. Being raised in the South, especially at that time, was really icky, however, I own my choices. Although I was coming into my teens in the mid-70s, I did not protest or fight against the racism in the south. There were many reasons for that, all fear based. I am not the activist personality type, but the fact remains that I participated in that system, if only by being silent except for what was expected.

My dad was English and a lot older than my mom. He was 45 when I was born, my mom was 29, so you can see the age difference. Mom was born and raised in Richmond, Virginia, the proud Capitol of the Confederacy. I remember her telling the story of Richmond in the fifties as she was growing up. I believe it was Broad Street that had a white side and a black side. If she needed to go to two stores on the black side, she would cross over go to the first door cross back to the White side, walk down and cross over to the black side to visit the second store and then return to the White side. That was the system, what was expected, stay in your lane.

The South needs healing, but I have not seen or heard how that can happen. I have never heard of anyone where I grew up addressing that the white folks and the black folks with the same last name—Jones, Carter, White, etc.—that some were once owned by the others. There is a place within a very few miles of the home where I grew up that is called Negro Foot. If that isn't icky enough, the story behind how it got that name, which has several versions, are all really icky. The one I remember from growing up is that a slave was caught with the wife of the plantation owner, and he was killed, chopped up, and parts strung up around the county as a lesson to any other slaves. Wikipedia also states that it was an amputation as a lesson not to run away again.

I am an only child. As children are want to do, I made myself responsible for the undercurrent of anger that was ever present between my parents. It took many years to understand and put together the full picture. I will just say that as a child, my father was not present emotionally., I don't think he was capable of it. British, stiff upper lip, he even told me that he built up the walls. Many years later, I learned that the walls do indeed protect you from what you don't want, but they also prevent anything that might be beneficial or contribute to you; they keep that out too. I think my dad missed out on a lot because he built those walls and kept them up. He told me he loved me and I believe that and I believe he believed that. But his parenting was to treat me as a small adult. It might sound like a good idea, but children are children, not small adults. I remember him telling me things like he was very worried about me expressing anger because he watched his mother and his sister with mental health problems, therefore, anger expression was not acceptable. That's a lot to put on a child; so, what I learned was that there was no safe place to express anger externally. The only safe place to express anger was internally, at myself,. and I became very good at it. Better, more cutting, faster to put myself down than anyone else. It can still be a knee-jerk reaction for me to go to that place, and hopefully, I've gotten faster at seeing that and catching it before I spend time going down that rabbit hole. But self-worth issues and not being good enough are the first things that I think I can remember.

My mother was a beautiful, perceptive soul who somehow made the choice to put herself through tremendous physical pain and died much too young at 57. The list of physical ailments was psoriasis, psoriatic arthritis, hypertension, and type 2 diabetes. The experimental treatments they put her through in the late seventies and eighties were devastating to her health, and I think of that price when I see the drugs that are advertised now. It is my point of view that before we come into this existence, we choose what we want to experience. So, my mom chose to experience incredible physical pain, and I chose the experience of having a mother who was in a lot of pain.

I have very dim memories of a couple of times when my dad was gone when I was really young. I figured out later that that moment was when they decided to stay together, but it was a very unhappy marriage. My mom was young, and she worked for a time when I was a baby. She was a social worker in our County of Hanover in Virginia, north of Richmond. She was an Aries and had a temper, and my dad would lose his mind when she would come home and say she got angry and quit her job that day. I think she was young and impetuous. She was the eldest of six children, so she certainly had her share of child-rearing before I came along. There was a divide with the family after she married my dad. I believe my grandmother's quote was, "How do you know he doesn't have bald-headed kids with glasses riding around the world in England and Europe and who knows where else?" My dad encouraged my mom to stay in touch and, sure enough, after there was a granddaughter, I am the first granddaughter, not the first grandchild as I was preceded by boys, their relationship improved. My mother and grandmother grew to be incredibly close over the last 20 years of my mother's life.

Going back to memories of when my dad was not at our house, many, many years passed before I discovered the truth. My father suspected that my mother had been taking money from his wallet; cash. He confronted her and she denied it so he set her up and caught her where she couldn't deny it. That began about 25 years of him being angry with her, shutting her out, treating her poorly at home and in public. It was a very long time for me to see them both as people. He was rigid, judgmental, and unbending. She was young and had had to be responsible in the family as the eldest. She went away to college and started working in Baltimore but then returned home to help the family when her dad was ill. She told my dad that she just wanted some cash to buy herself some treats. Dad, however, in his judgmental fortress, could not forgive. So, he shut her out until about a week before she passed away. He had regrets, and at the time, I had very little compassion for him because he was sad about what he had missed by his choice for 25 years. I was not forgiving about how he had treated Mama for those 25 years. Forgiveness did come to me a few years after his passing. It is sad on all sides for the missed time and opportunities, but it did show me that I can be different.

CHAPTER 7:

FINDING AND DEFINING
SELF-WORTH

So, self-worth is the first topic I would like to address. The South was really, really good at telling you what you did wrong, how you fell short, how you were not enough, or you were too much! You would be beaten down until you were small. Children should be seen and not heard. All the lessons. I spend a lot of time examining and working on the feeling of not being enough. I think the phrase that had the most impact on me was the question: "If I asked you to name all the things that you love, how long would it take for you to say yourself?" One thing I learned during the pandemic shutdown, as I was searching for the truth was that the one website that would give me the truth didn't exist because each person on this planet has their own truth. And just as we each have our own truth, we are each just as and no less valuable than every other person. You are no better than and no less than any other person consciousness on this planet, so the questions I have for you are, "Have you stepped into your light? Have you stepped into your truth? Have you stepped into your power?" Because if you still think that there are things missing or they don't feel quite right, there may still be work to do, but each one of you is a beautiful sovereign being. I love the Maya Angelou quote—"When you know better, you do better." Until you know better, please give yourself Grace for doing the absolute best you could at the time.

TRAUMA

It wasn't until 2023 when I went to a family reunion with all my first cousins and the ones who remain from the generation older than ours, that I discovered that I lived in the crazy family. Every single one of my first cousins is married to their first spouse. They are all sane and raised evidently with a good stable beginning. I chose to do some different work. I believe I have offered apologies to every one of my exes, but if any of y'all need to hear more or hear it another time, I will absolutely own my part of every relationship that I have had. I did not treat everyone kindly. I hopefully know better now and do better now.

When I was a freshman in college, I had my first romantic encounter with a woman and all of a sudden all the light bulbs went off. If I had known when I was younger that I was gay, all it would have given me was a name. I graduated from high school in 1980 and believe me there was no internet, there was no gay straight student alliance, there was nothing but Southern judgment of what an awful person you must be if you were gay. I didn't come out until my sophomore year in college, and there was a lot of drama trauma around that. From the time of earliest memory, being gay was judged as wrong. I don't know what the experience of being a person of color is, because I'm white, and I can sort of pass as straight. In what universe that is true, I'm not really sure, cuz to me, I always feel like I walk around with a big D in the middle of my forehead. Dyke! But sure, if you are completely unconscious, I can pass. People see what they want to see. Especially once I knew who I was, the constant microaggressions of language that people use was difficult. This was my experience growing up in a very different world than what we have now. I hope what we have now is better, but sometimes I think it is filled with just as much judgment of where you are supposed to fit. I do think that growing up gay in the South is one of my first experiences of trauma.

And at that time, this was not limited to the south. I remember in the early 90s living in New York City walking through Times Square hand in hand with my partner and the homeless guy screamed at us f*****. Now that's a lot on many levels, first we were in New York City, home of theater where we're all misfits and folks who don't fit in. So, you'd think that would have been a welcoming place! But no, in the early 90s, even the homeless people were judgmental and looked down on gay people. And, by the way, wrong gender on your insult! What a weird thing to be entitled about!

It took me a long time to understand also that the consequence of my mother becoming ill when I was a teenager. My dad presented to me that Mom was sick, she wasn't going to work anymore, and that he and I, namely me, would be responsible for everything in the house. I was expected to fix dinner and have it on the table by the time he returned from his job in Richmond. It made me sort of grow up a little, but mostly it meant that I could never ever say anything bad about my mom. She never complained, so she was the angel going through this ordeal. What I finally understood later is that made it so that I couldn't ask for what I wanted or maybe needed because she was sick. Again, I must stay small. I think my parents tried to let me be out on my own, becoming a young adult, and not "burden me" with her illness once I left the house. But, they would not tell me when she would be in the hospital. It didn't feel good to try to call home; Mom was the only one who ever answered the phone unless you gave the signal so my dad would answer. When Mom didn't answer the phone, I eventually learned to just call the hospital and they connected me through to her room. I know my dad did the best he could, but he must have been dealing with a lot because months before my mom passed away, it was a Sunday night, he heard a noise in the bathroom. He went in to find my mom on the floor so he got her up, cleaned her up, put her in the bed, and asked if she needed to go to the hospital. And my mother could not speak. Dad's response was to wait until the morning to take her into the emergency room. I was in my last semester of graduate school and met him at the hospital where I proceeded to tell him exactly what I thought of that choice. I know I was not kind, and I know that he probably was beating himself up more than I could ever do to him. Mom had a stroke so getting to the hospital quickly would have been one choice.

It was a very long time before I identified many of these experiences that I had as causing trauma. I was not sexually or physically abused. I didn't have experiences that some people relate about their childhood and awful experiences that they go through, so I didn't think that I had trauma. As a consequence of there not being a safe place outside my body to be angry or to place these emotions, I locked them in my body. She bore them forever. If you don't know about all the different types of therapy that are out there, please go take a look at what is available. I went through some somatic therapy to unlock what I had put into my body. I loved it because unlike talk therapy, I didn't need to know what it was. I didn't need to go back and re-experience it. I didn't need to sit in the puddle of poo and pick it up and look at it and smell it and agree that that was a pile of poo! I just needed to say yep, that was poo. Body, would you like to get rid of this, would you like to let go of this and find the movement that allows it to unlock and go away? If you haven't heard of IFS, internal family systems, it is something fairly new to me, but basically it looks at you as the whole person who is made up of many parts. These parts all exist at the same time, so it can be this and that at the same time, they can all be true at the same time. There are many, many modalities out there. There is so much free content available, especially on YouTube as a starting point. Find what works for you. I am aware that having medical coverage or the income to go to talk therapy or any other therapy is a place of privilege. Find what works for you. Maybe you start a group. I like having peace circles, whatever it is. There are so many paths, options, and things you can find meetup groups, Facebook groups. We live in an age where everything is usually just a few clicks away. Please find what works for you.

CHAPTER 8:

WE ALL HAVE GROWING PAINS

I hope that you see in me the person that I have been, the person I am now, and the person that I still strive to become. I like for things to be simple which does not mean always easy but simple. I love a good win - win - win! Can you feel in your body when something is either light for you or heavy for you? Most people, if you examine this, may find a physical indication or reaction that gives you information. Your body knows truth; your body is also wise and wants to heal. The biggest thing is for us to get out of our own way. This is not a workshop and I don't need to take you through finding that as there are so many resources available, but just know it is available to you to access the wisdom of your body to ask questions and to see what the answer is. Is it light? Is it expansive? Is it heavy? Does it make my body want to contract? If we ask questions about every single thing that we are faced with in this life, our body is there, ready to give us truth and guidance. So, ask questions, just stay in the questions.

You don't even necessarily have to have answers because if you decide on an answer, you let your ego, your mind, decide what something is without asking questions. Who knows where that came from. Questions, to me, feel expansive, whereas definitions feel constrictive. To ask questions, such as from Access Consciousness, what else is possible? What is possible that I've never even considered? Those are some small examples of questions so simple, just like your breath. So many things in your life can be solved with simple breathing, we have so many powerful tools that involve breathing! Something my body does all the time without me even thinking about it.

After I moved out from living with the other woman, I went through bankruptcy. I had created all sorts of debt and could not keep up anymore. I chose to walk away from the house and that was a fascinating process to watch. My ex was able to live in the house for several years rent-free. Because she had the rescue, the bank could not turn that property around without some major expense, so it kept getting sent to the bottom of the list for foreclosure. Eventually, it was in foreclosure and my ex found a donor to pay for the house and keep the rescue open. What was so interesting to me was my friends' reactions. I no longer had any obligations to the house, so I was fine with whatever was going to play out. My friends, however, were just irate that she lived there rent-free. It makes sense to be outraged, but it was amusing to me to see them so worked up while I really didn't care. I guess it is all about perspective and judgment and the need to be right. I appreciated their support; they saw the situation as unjust, but we had different opinions of the situation.

During this time, I was involved in the Ultra Endurance Cycling community. I was doing some races myself, but I also was on the crew for several Race Across America events. It went from Oceanside, CA, to Annapolis, MD, although the route has changed recently and now finishes in Atlantic City, NJ. During the second time I did the full race, I met a woman and we were attracted to each other. It was a fascinating experience to spend 10 days in a van together to bond and get to know each other. It was equal to a long-time dating crammed into that 10-day journey. When I returned to Florida, I began considering a transfer out west. It was my opinion that we would never know if the relationship might work unless we were physically closer. At that time, the farthest west my company had offices was Phoenix.

I transferred to the Phoenix office, and although the relationship didn't work in the end, I found that I really like living in the West. It is so interesting to me the differences between the coasts and the people there. I like the low humidity and the more open and relaxed outlooks from most people. I feel that I am just more comfortable here than in the South. Over the last 12 years, I have dated some but no one for more than six months. I have not attracted the right partner. I know I am not looking for a regular relationship or marriage. I feel that in those long-term relationships, the main goal often seems to be simply not wanting to rock the boat. Keep your peace and get along every day. I have been in those relationships, but it is not what I am looking for now. I am looking for a spiritual partnership, one dedicated to continuous growth and expansion of both partners. That will sometimes mean challenging each other, saying the uncomfortable thing. I first heard about this from Gary Zukav in his book, *Spiritual Partnership: The Journey to Authentic Power.* It has called to me ever since and is what I am looking for.

Why is a spiritual partnership important to me? My outlook is that I hope I learn something new every day. I believe our life here in this physical plane is about expansion and growth. Ray Kroc said, "As long as you're green you're growing, as soon as you're ripe you start to rot."

In other words, never stop growing! I find growth to be like plants, in fits and spurts. It may not be a steady continuous progress. It may take big leaps at times, followed by settling in and integration of growth. I think of nature, mountains, and the earth as solid and unmoving, until there is a sudden shift, whether it is an earthquake as two plates slide past each other, or a volcano that causes a total change in the landscape. Nature sort of sits in stasis until a sudden shift happens. It is not a steady progression, but big jumps followed by rest periods.

PART TWO:

DISCOVERING THE TOOLS TO CHANGE OUR WAY OF BEING

CHAPTER 9

GAINING PERSPECTIVE

Max Planck's insightful observation…

"When you change the way you look at things, the things you look at change."
Also attributed to Dr. Wayne W. Dyer

I once heard a dog trainer turn our perception of dog's separation anxiety around. Most of us view the dog's reaction to our leaving is the dog having anxiety that the person who cares for them is not here. We assume the dog is wondering… *Will we ever return? Who will care for them if we don't?* We consider that the dog sees the person as the pack leader and therefore is anxious when the leader is gone. What if our perception of the dog's behavior is wrong? What if instead the dog thinks that the person is the one the dog is responsible for? The dog looks at the way we deal with the world and thinks we are pretty poor dogs. We don't seem to know or sense when there is danger, therefore, from the dog's observation, we just are not good leaders. So, the dog has to step in where they see that we don't have the skills. The dog sees themself as the leader; they have to take care of the person in this world who cannot do it on their own. But our modern world is not a fair place to be a dog trying to be the leader. They don't necessarily understand cars, stop lights, or the internet. But they do know how to be safe. It is an unfair position to put the dog in—to try to lead the people in this overwhelming world.

So, if the dog is coming from this perspective, of course they are upset when their baby that they are responsible for leaves. Their baby goes out into the scary world where the dog can't follow and protect them. Of course, the dog is relieved when their person returns home because the person is now safe and back home. So, instead of the dog being anxious that you left because you are not there to protect them, they are anxious that they cannot protect you. A simple change in the way we look at the situation changes everything.

Perspective- like the drawing where an object looks like two totally different things- maybe a solid rectangle from one angle. From another angle 90 degrees away, it is a capital E. Like the quote says, change the way you look at things and the way things look will change. And nothing has happened; nothing has occurred to make this change. No outside force is causing this shift in your thinking or feeling. But, by shifting your internal thinking, by shifting your thoughts and way of looking at something, you change not just your thinking but your feelings about that thing. And the way your body reacts changes with your thoughts. A thought that used to give you fear and anxiety and that would make your body tense and reactive to the fear can become the one thing you are most grateful for in the world.

Perspective is what makes Radical Forgiveness work. *Radical Forgiveness* is a book by Colin C. Tipping, and it examines instances of people finding forgiveness in situations where many would find it understandable to never forgive. Stories like Immaculee Ilibagiza finding a way to forgive her Rwandan perpetrators of genocide who murdered her entire family. Hers is a most extreme story, and it is almost unbelievable what she found and how she could forgive these people. But her change in perspective not only allowed her to forgive but to thrive after the ordeal was over. Simply by changing how we look at something, we can alter everything. We can stop inflicting pain upon ourselves, start to find gratitude, and offer healing to our body.

Perception is so individual it is almost impossible to know what someone else sees. Is your color red that you perceive the same as mine? We really have no way of knowing. We all just go along in the world, gathering information, trying to figure out if your red is the same as mine. Like the painting that looks so different from right up close to pointillism where you have to back away and have some distance to see the points blend into the painting, many things in our experience look or feel different if we are right up close or far away. Just a simple change in perspective.

"A man was rowing his boat upstream when suddenly he saw another boat heading towards him. He shouted, 'Be careful! Be careful!' but the boat plowed right into him, nearly sinking his boat. The man became angry and began to shout, but when he looked closely, he saw no one in the other boat. The boat had drifted

downstream by itself. He laughed out loud. When our
perceptions are correct, we feel better, but when they are
not, they can cause us a lot of unpleasant feelings."
Thich Nhat Hanh

Let's say for the sake of argument that two people had the exact same traumatic upbringing. The same terrible childhood experiences, the same trauma, the same background. This is what makes people endlessly fascinating—one person will take the experience and become a victim. They become stuck and never move past the poor start in life. They never develop skills, never are able to better themselves. They stay in the same cycle forever. And you could argue that they have good reasons for staying that way. The other person uses the early experiences as motivation. They use those things that happened and that time as the reason to make change, to become healthy and thriving. They do not use the experiences as a reason or excuse, but as inspiration and motivation. That is simply a change in perspective. Same experience, but for one person, it keeps them down, and for another, it lifts them up.

How can you shift your perspective? How can you change how you look at something to make it a contribution to your life, not taking something away? I have had many experiences in my life that were not a lot of fun, that I may not have wanted to go through. But how do I make a judgment about what I want to keep and what I would want to get rid of? What would I change in the past and what would it mean for me right now? Since every single thing that has ever happened to me has brought me to where I am now, how do I pick what to get rid of? What effect would that have on me now? Can I even predict what ramifications changing something in my past might have now?

What if I did not struggle or regret or judge things that happened to me in the past? What if I was simply grateful for every single thing that happened since it brought me to right here, to right now, to this moment. I don't think I would take the chance on changing anything because what effects might that have on other things? It may not be easy to be grateful for each and every person and experience, but which choice feels better? To stay in judgment and regret and wish it was different? Or to be in total gratitude for what part it played in bringing you to right here, right now.

*Whether you think you can or you
think you can't, you're right.*
Henry Ford

From perspective comes empathy and compassion. Empathy is defined as the action of understanding, being aware of, being sensitive to, and vicariously experiencing the feelings, thoughts, and experience of another, or being able to understand how someone else is feeling. Compassion is a similar consciousness but with the added desire to make it better. I find it interesting that none of the definitions address the feeling. Empathy is the ability to feel what it feels like from the other person's perspective. Compassion is feeling empathy and taking action to make it better.

Why bring up empathy and compassion? Because a shift in perspective can totally shift how we perceive what that person is going through. When we see how someone else feels, we can change our opinion of why they act as they do. Maybe we see their behavior as not so much anger directed at us but as the blind hurt of a wounded child that they still carry. Maybe we can find love and empathy for them instead of being hurt and resentful. Maybe even just the smallest bit, maybe it is a tiny bit of space we can open up.

Abracadabra the original Aramaic meaning is I create as I speak. We often talk about how you create your own reality. This actually is a part of quantum physics. Called the observer effect, just the simple act of watching or observing any behavior or experiment alters the outcome. The most well-known quantum experiment was trying to determine if a photon was a particle or a wave. Called the double slit experiment, photons were passed through a plate with two slits or openings. With sending repeated photons, a pattern emerged that appeared to be like that of waves when they interfere with each other, such as could happen on the passing through the slits. They decided to watch and see what caused the interference and immediately the behavior of the photons changed to look like a particle.

While most prominent in quantum physics, the concept of an observer effect can also be found in other scientific fields, such as psychology and computer science, where the act of observing or studying a system can influence the outcome. And it is not just observing; it has been scientifically measured how our thoughts and feelings have a direct impact on our DNA and cellular function. The frequency of emotions has also been measured, Peace, Love, and Joy are at the top, with Guilt and Shame at the bottom, closely followed by Grief and Fear. We create our own vibration that we absorb throughout all our cells, and we also broadcast that frequency. Most of us, myself included, can be unconscious about our frequency. But what if we used our intention to create our reality, to create our day-to-day vibration? What if we create from a conscious place, an aware place, instead of on autopilot?

And, as Dr. Masaru Emoto's work shows, the vibration of what we put out into the world has an effect on our surroundings. Dr. Emoto did experiments with water by simply speaking words or putting labels on the water containers. He then froze the water and looked at the patterns under a microscope. It is astounding to look at the results. Positive vibrations like love and peace are coherent pleasant patterns, while the negative vibrations are misshapen, asymmetrical, and not very pretty to look at. So, when we add intention to the observer effect, it makes sense that we can create outcomes in our own lives. It can be created unconsciously by sitting in the same patterns we always have without conscious thought. It is just routine and by habit. Or, we can stay in a positive vibration like gratitude or peace or joy and create from that place.

Veda Austin has built on Dr. Emoto's work with water and images in the ice. She has new freezing and photographic techniques that reveal complex images in the water. She is able to take a snapshot of water in between water and ice states. It is truly remarkable what she has captured. It clearly shows a correlation with intention. This is where it is simple not easy to find that positive vibration and stay living in that vibration.

Water is vital to the physical human experience. We can go a few minutes without air, a few days without water, and a few weeks without food. Our bodies are 70% water so are our bodies affected the way the frozen water is? Do our bodies absorb the vibration we put into it? What vibration are you putting into yourself? What words are you putting into yourself? Simple not easy... how do you speak to you and what are you creating? Is it with intention or with the subconscious? What feels good and expansive? Stay in that space.

I hope to illustrate that your perspective is a powerful tool. Changing your outlook or perspective on a situation does not change the event, it does not change the experience you had, it only changes how you see and feel about it. That is a place of power. You took outside for information, experience, and input, and then made a choice about how you feel. In other words, you chose what vibration you wanted to respond with. You have all the choice, you have all the options available, and you can choose how you want to respond. That is power. You are a sovereign being who has the power to choose. For you, not for anyone else, but for the highest good of all. I hope that feels great in your body!

CHAPTER 10

JUDGMENT

Boy, this is a sneaky one. We use judgement all the time. As I have said, judgement comes up all the time in many ways. Our mind is on constant alert to whether something is a danger or not. It is making a judgment call if something is a threat. Our minds also work within all the lessons and programming we have picked up in our lives. Things we learned from our parents, school, other people, tv, and media, and all the information we are subject to from all sources. Much of this is subconscious and unquestioned. Do you examine what is true for you or are you coming from assumptions? It is pretty amazing just how much we function from habit and unquestioned thoughts. For me, besides the mind and unconscious thoughts, I was raised in the South where they live the very definition of passive aggressive. You say one thing to their face and another behind their back. I never really thought about it until I started to examine judgment. Once I did, I started to see so many places where I used judgment. For example, especially with a partner, I would keep all the text messages, because I would use them to prove that I was right. I would scroll back through to show what I said, what they said, and to show I was right. Have you ever heard the phrase "would you rather be right or would you rather be happy?" It is often used regarding relationships. It happens often so you can have many opportunities to practice! If someone did not remember the correct day of the week when something happened or anything where you or some-one does not have the facts correct. Now, listen to what happens.

- Did someone jump in to correct them?
- Did you?
- Was it necessary?
- Did correcting the fact make a difference?

How many times do we correct someone else and did it matter? Was the only thing accomplished to make you right? How did it make the person getting corrected feel?

Let's take a specific example.

You are frustrated because your partner did not take out the trash. In your frustration, you say "You never take out the trash!" Is that true? First gate - no, it is not true because they do take out the trash. Maybe not on your schedule, not at the second you ask or remind, but they do it. Didn't pass the very first gate. Another example, correcting someone's memory of a date or of an event. "It happened last Wednesday, not Thursday." Is it true? Maybe. Is it necessary? If it will affect a future schedule, yes, but does which day it happened in the past really matter? And finally, is it kind? If it does not affect the future schedule, does it matter to correct it? What will be accomplished? Do you feel right and justified? How does the other person feel?

So, it can be true, it may be necessary, but can you do it in the kindest way?

I believe our minds create judgment. It is a tool our mind uses to keep us safe. Everything the mind looks at; it is just trying to make sense of and put in one box or the other. Either something is safe or it is a threat. Once the mind has determined whether something is a threat or not, it can then make choices to either move toward safety or relax. The foundation of judgment seems to come from a good place—keeping the body safe and alive. As with many things in our human life, we have shifted to expand this idea of judgment to many other things. Many places in our lives foster judgement, such as government, religion, school. In a traditional classroom, there is only "one right answer." Another way to express judgment is whether you deem something right or wrong. For many years, we have lived with polarization that something has to be right/wrong, good/bad, true/not true, black/white. There is no in-between; we only have one extreme or the other. For me, I did some work to release the judgment I was carrying.

Judgment can apply to so many things. Judgment while driving a car to make safe choices, while shopping to make sure items meet you and your family's needs, in so many everyday situations. All day we make determinations and make choices based on those. Many, if not most, of these choices are happening unconsciously. The mind is so fast that it has formed an opinion about safety within moments, not even seconds, of a new encounter. It is my opinion that it is only when groups or entities start to make global judgments that the intention gets skewed and priorities get lost. So much of judgment is "other." We decide who is like us and who is not. If someone is identified to not be of our tribe or community, then they are other. And other can be a threat. But what if we could approach all of this from a different perspective. What if we took the information our minds come up with and then chose? We often forget the choosing part and operate from autopilot or past experiences. So, I suggest not that we get rid of judgment because I am not sure it is possible or even desirable for the mind to stop making judgments. What I am suggesting is that we take the information that our minds give us and then choose how to respond instead of react. We can get the message from our minds that the car that just cut us off is a jerk and it scares us. Reacting may look like honking or following or any other road rage choices. But, using empathy and compassion, what else is possible? Could you envision that the other driver is in an emergency situation? Or on their way to the hospital or just any possibility? Could they maybe be just a jerk? Sure, but if you are in control of your choices, what makes you feel better? Seeing the other driver as a jerk or seeing them as a fellow human going through stuff and maybe not making the best choices.

Judgment can be internal or external. I have so far been discussing all external examples of judgment. Making a determination if something is a threat or not is all motivated by external stimulus. We can judge ourselves internally as well. We decide if we are worthy or not, if our behavior was "good" or "bad", if we made the right choice or not. Internal judgement is usually something never talked about. Part of judging myself is the shame, the point of view that what I did is so bad, I never tell anyone.

Brené Brown and her work has had a huge impact on me. She is a researcher in vulnerability, empathy, courage, and shame. Shame has been a big lesson for me. In her work, Brené used an example that fit me and my growing up perfectly. She was talking about shame and guilt. If a child has an experience at school, maybe called out unfairly, teased by a teacher, or if they are caught doing something they shouldn't, they can have a couple of reactions. The child who comes home and talks about what happened and complains they were treated unfairly may feel guilt, but not shame. This child did not take on what happened as an identity. Another child, after being shamed in front of the classroom, does take that on as an identity. They do not speak about what happened, but it is on their mind and they replay what occurred over and over and ruminate over it. The first child could be guilty—"I did something bad," but the second child has now judged themselves to be bad, lacking, wrong, and shameful in some way. "I am bad." I was the second child. I took on what others told me I was responsible for. I took on the blame for the anger in my home which was really just between my parents. But without anyone talking about it, without explanation or showing me a positive way to deal with my emotions, I went inward. I suspect all of these reactions are influenced by each individual and their personality types, personal biases, even astrological signs, etc, meaning only that there is a huge gamut of reactions and individual responses to a situation. For me, I put my blame and anger inside, so that is my well-worn pathway. It must be my fault because I am bad. Shame, lack of self-worth, what I have learned is that even though this will always be my go-to, the pathway I am most familiar with, just by recognizing, naming, and speaking shame and worthiness, that takes away their power. Shame does not exist in the light and in conversation. It relies on silence and judgment, remaining hidden is the only way to maintain power. So, is it really as simple as speaking about your mistakes, foibles, weaknesses? If it is with someone who respects you, is a safe place for you, and will honor your being then yes, bringing these things into the light will take away their power.

*What words do I use? How do I speak to myself
and how do I speak to and about others?*

It has been scientifically measured that the thoughts and emotions we choose have a direct impact on our own DNA and cellular function. We used to think that once we grew up and the brain was mature, it was set and not changeable. So, injuries would be permanent for example. What the new science shows is the brain is remarkably adaptive and able to heal as well as shift functions to different areas of the brain. This has opened the field of neuroplasticity which studies how the brain makes changes. Our thoughts even influence our DNA. Our thoughts that we focus on actually create biochemical changes that happen in our body. Our DNA is not fixed. Our DNA is constantly listening to its external environment and then it's making changes. I suppose if we think of survival, this is important. The strongest genes promote the healthiest individuals who have a stronger opportunity to not just survive but thrive. So, our thoughts and feelings don't just impact our thoughts and feelings. There are physiological changes that can be measured.

The Simple not Easy task is to focus on positive thoughts and feelings. Can you sit in the place where your thoughts make you feel good? And, I do not believe it is necessary to be in "perfect" thought 24/7 every second of every day. It does not have to be complicated or use Affirmations. It can be as simple as sitting and breathing, feeling your heart and love. Stay in that moment as long as you can. Your mind will wander, it will go off with thoughts, but if you keep coming back to feeling love, staying in your heart, things will shift. Feelings are just that, emotions in the body that give us information. It is only when we start to attach judgment with our thoughts that we then assign them as positive or negative. And I think that they only really affect us when we stay stuck in the feeling. Feelings just are. Physiologically, feelings only have a biochemical impact on the body for 90 seconds or so. That is the most intense part and often begin to ease. If you have an emotional attachment to something that happened 10 years ago, that emotion is in your thoughts and your associations with that event. You are carrying around that burden well after your body has moved through the emotion. How does that feel? Have you locked that experience, that feeling into your body because it could not flow through? Which choice is more expansive?

So, feel all the feelings. Experience all the emotions fully. Experience them without resistance. I have been able to observe this in myself. Say, for example, that I have a pain in my body. We often focus on it, worrying it, keeping our attention there but with resistance. "I have this pain and I don't want to." If I work to allow: yes, it hurts, and I totally feel that. I don't resist or avoid. When I spend a few minutes just allowing, I find that the pain often lessens. It is in the resistance that we cause ourselves the most harm. Like the Serenity Prayer—can you change it, yes or no? If yes, great, you can take action, but if no, can you let go of the emotional attachment?

When I say feel all the feelings, it has actually taken some effort on my part to totally feel them. And I mean all the feelings. Joy, sorrow, grief, gratitude. When I am conscious and aware, I intentionally go in and concentrate on feeling. It does not take a long time, but I try to be in my body and feel all the sensations from that emotion, the "good" ones and the "bad" ones. Really feel the depth of the emotion. Precisely, because they only last a short time in the body, grab the opportunity! Feel all of it! And certainly, look for and ask what that emotion is here to show you or what can you learn or see new information. To be clear, thinking about what happened to bring up the emotion or any other processing which may start happening after the 90 seconds of physical response is not in and of itself a bad thing. It is hanging onto the emotions after that. It is only when you worry and revisit the emotion over and over again that you create the potential for storing that in the body and never releasing the emotion. It is also easy to tell where you are. Does the thought of someone or something in your past bring up an emotional response? When you think about it, do you feel the emotion again just as strongly? That emotion tells you that you are still attached and have not let it go. If you can revisit the thought without the emotion, you have released attachment and it is now another one of your experiences in life, without the emotional burden.

Buckminster Fuller was an architect, writer, inventor, and philosopher. One of his areas of interest was systems. He became interested in the idea of trim tabs. In fact, the newsletter that is still published by his Institute is called Trim Tabs. Trim tabs are parts of the rudder of a ship or on the wings of a plane. They do perform the function of small final adjustments or trims to stay level or on course. The context that I first heard about them was in turning a large ship. Once in motion, the water puts force onto the rudder that will make it want to stay in place. Because the force is so great, in order to turn the rudder, they came up with these trim tabs. The smaller trim tab is easier to move and creates a disruption in the force of the water against the rudder. Once there is a disturbance to the water and the forces on the rudder are reduced, you can move the full rudder. The metaphor is that using a small disruption or change can create large scale change. Why do I bring this up? Because you don't have to try and do it all at once, regardless of what we are talking about. Do you want to make a change? Say, you want a new job that makes you happier. You could quit your current job and jump into a job search. That could work if you have savings and an emergency fund, but if not, you can get small and simple. Do you know what you want to do? If yes, great - what are the steps to get you there? If no - how can you start? Can you talk to friends and family and get feedback on their thoughts of your strengths? Can you do research? Find someone who is doing what you want to do and talk to them. You can make small moves to open opportunities and get ready for the big move. Give yourself some room and grace. The time of disruption at first may not be comfortable, but if you have a clear vision and the desire to grow and heal, you will find your way to peace and expansion.

CHAPTER 11:

BECOMING RESILIENT

Resilience is an interesting trait. It is tied to other things like authenticity and empowerment, but even in the presence or absence of those, some people become resilient, and some do not. For me, resilience is the knowledge gained by going through experiences, learning, and coming back to try again. It is getting back up after you are knocked down. Some folks seem to naturally have this ability to move forward after a setback. Some folks do not. If they get knocked down, they tend to stay there, tend to stay a victim who does not have the strength and ability to get up again. So, if you are one of the people that does not have the inherent strength and resilience, I think you can develop it or at least become aware and attuned to it to help you. Another way to describe resilience is the tolerance of the fact that things will not always be great. But, the only constant is change, so if things are not great right now, you have experienced things, and you know it will change. You have a little space, a little tolerance built up that it is only temporary and will change again, to hopefully better. You can think of this in other literal terms, say a milder allergy maybe to cats. If you are around them all the time, you get desensitized and you don't have symptoms. If you go away for a few days, you may be more sensitive, but more exposure will reduce the symptoms. Same for tolerance—you can build tolerance if you don't resist, stay in the uncomfortable place, accept what is, and look for signs of how to make change.

Let's say some event has happened to you, and it is deflating or defeating to you. Does this resonate with some event in your past? Does it remind you of or feel like something that you went through in your childhood? I know for me that when I have a big emotional response to something it is rarely that one isolated event. It brings up my feelings from another time in my life - shame, lack of self-worth, any of the well-worn pathways for me. Maybe you have a loss of some sort now, like a job or maybe having to move; something that is a loss but nothing like what you went through when you lost a parent or some other huge loss. The current event is not that big, but especially if I have not done my healing work, it will feel exponentially bigger because it resonates with that unhealed part of me. Even if I have done some healing work, it can still feel like an outsized reaction if it brings up and resonates with your past. Through taking a moment and examining your feelings, see if it feels like something else you remember and ask some questions. It will help tease out all the components of what is going on. For me, it allows me to take some time, not react emotionally, examine my stuff, and try to see the other person's side. It takes a situation that could feel overwhelming to me because it is so big and breaks it down into all the contributing pieces. I can examine each piece and separate out the parts and my reactions. All this is simple not easy. When you are in the middle of an emotional reaction, slowing down, not reacting, stepping back to examine the response, that all sounds good, helpful, productive, but when you are in the middle with strong feelings swirling around, it is not easy to create that moment of space. But if you do, if you catch it before you react, if you can pry open just that one tiny moment, Celebrate! That is a huge accomplishment! You did something differently. It may not seem like a big deal, but it really is. We have neural pathways in our brain; I like the hiking trail example. There are the often walked, wide smooth paths we have walked before. We have been doing the same thing or having the same thoughts so we just increase the ease of that path. To do something differently, you are hacking your way through bushes and overgrowth to create a new pathway. It is hard going, and the next time you meet that fork in the road it is easy to slide down the old path. It is much easier going on the old path. The new path still requires attention to stay on it, to stay aware and intentional to be in the new pathway. Eventually, the new path becomes a wider, smoother trail and easier to travel.

I also believe resilience is tied to our ability to let go and move on. I spoke of Brene Brown's work on shame. Our response to shame is tied to whether we can be resilient or not. I'll use her example of children in school and whether they have shame over an incident at school or not. The child who comes home and talks about what happened most likely will be more resilient. They are more able to say I did something bad instead of I am bad and taking all that on. And in silence, because shame only exists in silence. Resilience seems to be a healthy reaction that says, I did something bad, but I am not a bad person. I see the lesson, and I can forgive myself and move on.

Resilience also has a contribution from safety. This is elusive and hard to pin down, as what is safety to one person is not safety to another. If, at minimum, you can feel safe within yourself, that goes everywhere! If you know that you can handle anything that comes at you because you are strong, capable, and adaptable, I believe that you are resilient and feel safe within yourself. Whatever it is that gives you strength and safety - is it home? Is it your mom or your family? One area of safety can expand to others and show you how you are capable of bouncing back. To be clear, being safe and resilient does not mean you will not experience challenges, that you will be protected from "bad" stuff. It does not, you are human living on Planet Earth, you will face challenges, struggles, heartbreak, you name it. What it does mean is that you are equipped to face them, deal with them, and move on. You have a stable foundation, and you know you will be fine, regardless of what happens. Remember, you are a divine being and have been through hard times in the past. Give yourself grace, one foot in front of the other, and move forward.

One foot in front of the other reminds me of a lesson I learned from my mom. Mom was ill for many years, and I remember her telling me one day that sometimes looking up and ahead was too much. She had to get really small, and she couldn't look at the big picture. She couldn't look at it all because it's too big, too overwhelming. She would get really small and look straight down at her feet. She would look as she placed one foot in front of the other. She kept her head down and just saw one step after one step.

I had been working a desk job and wanted to get out and get active. I went back to riding my bicycle as it was something I enjoyed and had done a lot as a kid. It was not easy challenging myself and getting back in shape. I lived in the Washington DC area, and one day I was faced with the hill to climb up to Mt. Vernon on the trail I often took. I had attempted it once before and had to turn around. My mom's words came back to me, and I just put it in the lowest gear and kept watching my feet moving forward. Just looking down, seeing each rotation as progress. Eventually, I was at the top and could look up! If that's all you can do, please acknowledge that that is progress. You are moving forward. You are taking small steps but you are moving, you are doing your thing, you are going forward. That is amazing.

TRIGGERS

I see triggers or trigger warnings a lot today. A trigger in the mental health area means something that brings an emotional response that has its origins or resonance from the past. My interpretation is that a trigger is anything that you have an emotional response to. That emotional response gives you information. The response lets you know you are still attached to the past, and it still has an effect on you today. It says the past event has not been addressed and healed, or if you have done previous work on it, that you are ready for more, different, or deeper healing of that issue. If you haven't done the healing work on an emotional response, it makes sense that you will try and avoid the situation again and feel those old feelings. It is your mind, body, ego—however you look at it—trying to keep you from hurt. That is what a large part of our human existence is—I chose to come here and experience things, I forget what a divine being I am, and my body and mind try to keep me from hurt. I believe growth and expansion come from these experiences that stretch us, addressing and examining experiences, and then healing, whatever that looks like. It may be setting boundaries, choosing who, when, and how people have access to you and your time, or just letting go and moving on.

But the technique of avoidance, desiring to be notified of potential triggers, staying away from people or situations that bring up the old feelings, is very limiting and disempowering to me. It is not easy to do the work, but if you go through life just trying to not be put in triggering situations as you go on living, do you add more of these to your life? Will it eventually add up to being debilitating and restricting you to your home or some other small comfort zone? Do you make yourself smaller and smaller to avoid all triggers? That does not feel good to me. So, if you look at and examine the triggering event or situation, can you find ways to heal, let go of attachment, and remember you are not the same person who went through a traumatic event? You can make different choices now.

So that is my opinion on triggers. You choose how you respond. You can get small and try to avoid or hide from anything that feels like the old event, or you can meet the issue, see what it is here to show you, and learn and grow. Simple, not easy but look at which one is open, expansive, and growing and which is restrictive, confining, and contractive. What feels good? You are in control, you have choice, and you do not have to be held hostage by these experiences. Even in some of the worst experiences, people have found ways to look at it and see the lesson it gave, the gifts it brought, and the opportunity to grow and expand.

Attributed to Laurie Buchanan – "*What you are not changing, you are choosing.*" Meaning if you are not making changes, you are continuing to choose your current state. So, not making a choice is in fact choosing. Not choosing, not making a choice, is also choosing. You have just chosen stasis. And maybe that is required sometimes. But staying in one place, doing the same thing day after day, staying static, is also choosing to not grow.

Be clear and intentional about your choices. Anything that you keep doing without examination is still a choice, it is just choosing not to make change. And that may be working great for you, just have awareness. It is surprising to me sometimes to realize I have been doing the same thing over and over again without thinking about it. Maybe I will make the same choice, but I now have more information and know why I choose a or b. Goldie Hawn and Kurt Russell have never gotten married and have been together for more than 40 years. Goldie is quoted as saying, "We've done just perfectly without marrying. I like waking up every day and knowing I have a choice—and Kurt does, too. We choose each other, again and again." That boils it down to its simplest possible essence—I choose you. I choose you today. And do that every day! Choice can seem big, overwhelming, such a commitment, but it can be as simple as just saying yes to you every day. Yes, I matter. Yes, what I want is important. Yes, I GET to choose me today.

RESILIENCE

Maybe resilience is the ability to remember; remember that you have gone through tough times before. Remember that they are not permanent. Remember that you got through this before. Remember that it looks and feels overwhelming and it won't change, but it will change. Remember that it is only temporary to feel this way. Resilience is the ability to get back up again and again. And that ability gives you choice to expand. To try again. Look at sports. If the group dynamic is not resilient, then they fold when they get down in the score and just get through it. If they are resilient, they can fight back, never give up, and maybe win the game. And after you have that experience a few times, you develop the muscle to try again and try again, then maybe you expand and try something new. New input, new outcomes, and those are never failure. Outcomes only show the information that was good and I want more, or it didn't feel good and I don't want more. No judgment, just awareness of what I liked, what was helpful or felt expansive. Then with that information, you know to keep doing more or try something new. I think this newer idea of resilience can serve us well. Not like the greatest generation who we called resilient, but it was more of no choice. They kept going when they were depressed, beaten down, and faced continued adversity. They were resilient in that sense, but it was not with a sense of kindness to yourself. It was survival. They just kept doing it because they had no choice. If they didn't plow the fields, there was no food. But now, with the knowledge that we have, what if we can develop resilience while also honoring our needs and wants and emotional health? Wow, that is a powerful combination for growth and expansion.

Another example of resilience is actors, dancers, or anyone who has to audition. I watched and talked to performers when I was in NYC. I observed that talent and success in auditions were not necessarily related. Performers go to audition after audition after audition. I heard stories of these casting calls where you see the same people you were just competing against on another audition. I heard a story of a friend who called her childhood friend to bring her some shoes she had forgotten to her at the audition. The friend walked in the room with the shoes but couldn't find her childhood friend because everyone in the room looked alike. The phrase back then was, well, you may be one in a million, but in New York City there are seven of you! Can you imagine what it takes to show up day after day and keep getting told no? I saw performers who were so talented but the grind of daily rejection was too much, and they left town. Other performers who were maybe not as talented, but had that resilience to get up and audition day after day after day stayed and eventually would land a part. Different paths for all of us, but resilience is a trait, skill, or asset that helps every day but especially in crisis. And we all face crisis at one time or another. That is the human existence. How you get through it, how you get up tomorrow, and how you respond to adversity is up to you. Is it just a tough time and you will be better in the future and continue growing or expanding? Or is it too big, too overwhelming, and you get small and timid and contract? Maybe that is what you need right now, today, and you will be better tomorrow. The path is not a straight line, but as long as you make progress, as long as you are not in the same place as a year ago—Awesome!

Where else can you find things to support your growth in resilience? Sports may provide support. You didn't make your shot yesterday, but you have more opportunities in the next game. You may lose a game, but there is another chance in the next one. I have heard athletes talk about hard losses. What I find in common is they will stay in grief or mourning or just being down, but only for a short time. Coaches preach to have short memories. You can't carry the last game into this one today. Another way to put it—let it go! Don't be attached that the past and what happened. You make a new start in a new game. What a terrific skill to learn!

Where else can you find support for your resilience? Friends? Good friends love you no matter what happens. They may have another perspective that is helpful for you. They may just give you love and support to get over a hard experience. How you work through it does matter. If you need to stay in the "what happened" space, retell the story, stay in the energy and vibration of the experience, do that, but not permanently! If your friends give you the space to rehash it, but then they help you move on, perfect. If your friends just want to retell the same story, stay in the past event, keep rehashing the same thing over and over, maybe examine if they are helping you grow and change, or just stay the same and keep stagnant. Life always wants to grow and expand. What will support that in your life?

Friends, sports, church—these are all places where you can get support and grow. Most importantly, they are community. The need for community and connection is vital to health and wellbeing and is important for overall health. Just look up the effects of social isolation. It affects mental health, emotional health, and physical health. Statistics show increased risk of heart disease, weakened immune system, and lack of exercise and activity. All that from feeling alone? From not having contact and support from people? It shows who we are as human beings, animals that evolved in communities because that brought safety, cooperation, and food. And so, connection is required for our health. It is best in person, but even online, community is connection. Find what works for you; family, made family, your people.

CHAPTER 12

SNE TOOLS AND TECHNIQUES

MUSCLE TESTING:

This tool is required to access the information from your mind and tune into your body. This is the foundation of getting answers from your body.

In addition to, or in place of, if you haven't yet found the sensation of expansion/contraction in your body, is muscle testing or applied kinesiology. It is fascinating to look that up and see information on the internet. The medical profession seemingly, across the board, says this is bunk. Muscle testing does not work; it is unreliable. Honestly, I find that astounding given my personal experience, and then you can find countless videos and articles talking about this tool. Muscle testing can be used with a facilitator or by yourself. I leave it up to you to determine if this is a tool that works for you or not.

THE FACILITATOR TECHNIQUE:

This is done with two people and the concept is to have the person being asked the questions hold out their arm horizontally. The questioner says a true statement like "say my name is Ellen." They then put pressure with a couple of fingers on my arm and press down. The pressing does not have to be hard, but the amount applied should be consistent from question to question. When my body states or hears the truth, my arm will lock and not be pushed down easily. If I am asked to say "my name is Susan", my arm will easily be pushed down. Practitioners say truth makes your body strong and a lie makes your body weak. Why does science say this is bunk? I will let you ask your own question—does this tool make me feel strong and empowered or does it not work and is useless? You know the answer for you.

THE SWAY METHOD:

Stand up, solid on your feet, hold something—a supplement, food, etc.—and ask if your body wants this object. When I do this, my body will sway immediately forward toward it as a yes, backward away if it is a no. There are also techniques where you use your fingers. You form a circle with one finger and thumb. You can either interlock your other circle of finger and thumb, or just use a finger. Ask a question and if it's true, you won't be able to break the circle. If a lie, you will push through the circle with little resistance.

Now, one big caveat to using that tool is that the info you get is only as good as your questions. I often ask what my body wants and also what my body needs, but even further is this good for my body? These can be the same answer or they can be in conflict. Consider this if you are using the tool. You can ask global questions like "Do I need to ask more questions?" "Have I asked all the questions I need to?" Please use this as a tool, use it as a guideline, but also be in your empowerment, use discernment, and have grace with yourself. Sometimes I have great sessions, but if I am frustrated, getting answers I don't believe or feel are right, I stop. Give yourself grace and either tune into your body again, as you may have not been speaking to your body, or come back again later. My mind will get in the way and insert itself if it can. "Thanks, honey, now please sit down for a while so I can talk to my body." Be aware and feel good about the information you are getting. Make sure that if it is true, you know who or what is giving the information. And decide that it resonates and feels true for you.

VISUALIZATION:

I learned this when I heard about visualization and the brain. The Silva Method has been around for a long time. You can see athletes prior to their event visualizing. The one I remember most is the skiers. You can watch them before their run going through the course in their mind. There is science behind this as it has been studied for some time. Studies show that the brain does not differentiate between an actual experience and an imagined experience. This is why visualization works because your brain has the same experience whether it is a real scenario or an imagined one. So, if your brain has this power, what are you feeding it? I used to be as good as anyone at self-deprecating humor, putting myself down. From the first time I heard about this, I changed the way I speak. I stopped speaking negatively. It does take some time, but just notice when you slip back. If this is something you want to try, just listen. Listen to what you say. Try to make it positive all the time. If you slip, just notice, give yourself grace that you are trying, and go on. Eventually, it will be like a new habit; you are so used to it you stop having to be conscious about it. And, if you stick with it, eventually the voice in your head gets more positive too. And eventually, you will notice quickly that the voice in your head is not positive. Is what it is saying true? Probably not. Mine is motivated by fear, by lack, by insecurity. I don't believe that is who you really are, that is not your true essence, but the mind doing its best to keep your body safe and well.

- Does it feel good?
- Which way feels better?

- Speaking positively or negatively?

Do what feels better.

A favorite tool of mine to use is one of Rumi's quotes. "Before you speak, let your words pass through three gates. Is it true? Is it necessary? Is it kind?"

That last one is a big deal for me. Is it kind? How do I speak to myself and others; is it kind? I would personally rather be kind than right. Jay Shetty at the end of his *On Purpose* podcast asks a series of questions with the last one being, "If you could pass one law for the whole world, what would it be?" For me, the three gates would create great change. What could happen if we only spoke kindly to others and to ourselves?

Finally, remember the meaning of abracadabra? I create as I speak. You are casting spells with your language. Your words have power. Feel the energy difference between saying "I am love" and "I am bad." I picked up from Access Consciousness the phrase "All of life comes to me with ease and joy and glory." I say that 10 times to myself very first thing in the morning when I wake up and last thing at night before I go to sleep. That is the vibration I end and begin my day in. How does that feel?

TUNE IN:

Our bodies are always giving us information. I have found why energetic sensations in the body are called subtle energies or the subtle body. Goosebumps are our body giving feedback, often in response to an energy. We talk about the hair on the back of our neck standing up. Without the mind being involved, your body is giving information. Now, imagine that sensation but the intensity much less. You can feel these subtle sensations in your body, but for me, for so many years, I was in my head or numbing or just not aware. It takes time, attention, and consistency to tune it but what a resource. With practice, you will notice the subtle energy in your body as much as goosebumps. As I said in the section about learning the yes and no feedback from your body, there is so much information available. There are many ways to tune in, but most are getting quiet and listening. You have to get past the mind running, running, all the time and hear more. You will be richly rewarded for this work though. Sensation, information, feedback on a constant basis is available. I will say, the biggest step though is not just tuning in but taking action. If you do get successful in getting this information from your body, please do act on what it tells you. For example, on your way home from work, you clearly get the message to turn where you normally don't. It is strong and clear to "turn here." You can get into your head about it and use your wonderful problem-solving mind to say, "That's not my usual route. I don't see a good reason to turn here." Any of the justifications your mind uses. But you got this information. Clearly, strongly. If you follow the guidance and turn here, you will never know what might have happened if you go your usual way. But be aware of the magic. Maybe your unexpected turn takes you home uneventfully and you think, I don't know why I was prompted to do that. Go on faith. Your body is truthful, you honored what was suggested, and that is all you know. Is that all you need to know? Or sometimes, you stumble on something new, just what you were looking for, or a contact that can change your future. Who knows? But if you disregard the information and take your usual path, you will never know what could have been different.

BE PRESENT:

Oh, this one is so simple. It seems so easy to say be present, but how long does it take for you to not be present. Your mind wants to go to the past or the future or anywhere other than this moment. Worrying has been described as being in the past and anxiety has been described as being in the future. Either place is not being here in this moment. Simple not Easy - stay in the present moment. A quick way to get into this moment is breathing. While you focus and concentrate on your breathing, you are only in the present moment. Because your body will breathe without our conscious effort, it is easy to slip out of the moment. Concentration on your breath is bringing you to this present moment. Find the breathing technique that works for you. There are so many types of breathwork and tools out there. You can make it really simple. Feel the air moving in your body, maybe at your nose and nostrils, fill your belly with air so it goes deep and fully fills your lungs, and then exhale. Maybe you would like to concentrate on the full cycle, because breathing is not just inhale - exhale. It is really inhale - pause - exhale -pause. Honor the full cycle. Every time you remember to take even one breath, you have created just that tiny bit of space.

Whatever you find that keeps you present, hold on to that. I find even if I try to stay present, I wander and will have to come back time after time after time. That's the deal! I have so much in life every day to keep me not present; I scroll social media, watch YouTube, or TV shows. But, with inspiration, motivation, and consistency, I can create a different well-worn pathway that gets easier. A big example I have had in my life lately is my very special dog Jasmine. I have had her since she was a baby, and we have the most incredible connection. She truly is one of the sweetest creatures on the planet. She has taught me so much. She has had health issues and is now 12 years old. I realized a few months ago that my anxiety about her health was not good for her. I was watching her obsessively and noticed every single little wheeze or cough, and I ran through all the worst possible scenarios in my head. She got really quiet and seemed depressed. I finally decided to get a companion, hoping it might help Jasmine and me. I was totally guided to a dog who was not the one I thought I wanted to see. I wound up with a senior Chihuahua who has been the perfect addition. She is quiet, not yappy like many little dogs, and has brought life and joy to our lives. Jasmine seems happier and more alive. It has honestly gone better than I had hoped for. And maybe the biggest impact has been because I am not in that worrying energy, Jasmine is lighter. It taught me to be present. Now, every day if we wake up together, I am grateful. Just love. I only pay attention to today. What happens tomorrow happens then, I have no control nor will ruminating over it make it different. It will only bring down my energy and vibration.

Simple, but not easy.

EXAMINE CONTROL:

For many of us, so much is happening it makes us feel insecure and afraid because we have no control over external things. People are different and have different reactions to this sense of not having control. Some will be tyrannical in their own home and dictate how everything goes because it gives them an area of control. This could take so many forms, but it is all about trying to ease the fear. If you feel out of control, exercising control in one area or part of your life is a way to address the fear. But, it rarely works, because it is like treating a symptom, not the cause. The cause is the fear, and it is not eased by controlling others. For me, only faith helps with feeling like I have no control. For the reality is, the only thing I have control over is me, and more importantly, my actions and reactions. I never really did have control over anything else. It was an illusion, or the same hill I kept trying to climb, but I never did have control over anyone or anything outside of myself. I can't change what outside event has occurred to me. I am only in control of how I react, or hopefully respond. Reaction is the immediate knee-jerk response. Responding takes some time, reflection, and discernment of what feels most expansive in the situation.

MEDITATION:

It seems like such a good idea. It's so simple, just sit quietly and empty your mind. Sure, simple but not easy to sit and not think. Thoughts fly around anyway. Thich Nhat Hanh is credited with saying that in meditation, it can be enough to just sit and smile. That is certainly simple, but not easy to simply stay in that space. You also often hear to create your space, an altar, candles, incense, many things, but the first requirement for a meditation space, in my opinion, is a safe space. I have never heard this stressed as important before, but I think a safe place is absolutely required. Often, not always, but often when you meditate, you close your eyes. This is probably a bigger deal for some people than others. You know, some folks are not comfortable sitting with their back to the door. Depending on what works for you personally, closing your eyes is more or less of a big deal. For me, for example, it is hard to meditate in my car. There are many things that can happen, people approach my car etc., so it is not a safe and comfortable space for me. You don't have to close your eyes; there are meditations where you concentrate on the flame of a candle. If you have tried meditation and it has not been successful, you haven't done it wrong. You just haven't found the meditation that works for you. What that is can change over time. There are guided meditations, music meditations, binaural beat meditations, just a ton of resources. And there are so many because there are so many different people. See if you can find the one that really helps you. If you go to yoga class, your couple of minutes at the end in corpse pose is a meditation. Maybe if you sit under a tree in nature and concentrate on your breath for two minutes, five minutes. If you have never done it before, see how it feels. Do you feel just a tiny bit more calm, peaceful? Please be kind to yourself as you search for the type that resonates for you. If one type doesn't work or you can't sit immediately for 20 minutes, no big deal. You haven't found the one for you, keep looking, see what is available close to you for in person. Make sure it is somewhere you feel safe, comfortable, and at peace.

How is your suitcase? You know, the one we all carry with all the past experiences, slights, hurt, resentment, guilt, just life that we are still carrying. You know, if you are carrying something that has an emotional charge, if when it comes to mind, you have an emotional reaction in your body. If when you think back to an event, if you can still experience the emotions then you are still carrying that emotion with you, all the time, adding to all the other experiences you are carrying. Is it heavy? Does it feel good? What if you could leave the emotion behind? What if you didn't have to carry it? You can, and it can be as easy as saying, "I choose to set this down and leave it behind." And later when you think back, if you don't feel the emotion, you have done it! You have set it aside. Now, I know this seems way too easy, like not possible. It is, because what you are setting aside is not the event, it is the emotion around the event. That is all true; it is what happened.

What you are setting aside is your attachment to the event. The attachment is where the emotional connection comes from. If you get to the place where you can say, "I cannot change what happened to me. I have been carrying the burden of that event for a long time. I choose to let go and set aside what no longer serves me." You still have all the gifts and learning and knowledge gained from the experience, but now without the emotional burden. You have created just a little space for something to heal. If you revisit this and find an emotional reaction, you did not fail.

Sometimes a part of us is ready to let go, but another part is still holding on. Honor all the different parts of you and ask if the part that wasn't ready to let go would like to let go now, would it like to join the party. Please honor the answer. If that part is not ready yet, there is nothing wrong. You now have more information. You can ask questions. You can talk to that part, you can listen, ask what that part needs, make sure that part knows it is loved and safe just as much as any other part. Just like people, each part wants to be seen and heard. Once it is acknowledged—seen and heard—then it will often be ready to let go as well. All you are doing is loving and honoring all parts of yourself, getting coherence and unity amongst all of you. Some parts may be ready right now, but some may not be ready yet. With love and intention, they will be. In their own time, on their own schedule, they will be ready to let go.

RESISTANCE, ALLOWING, AND ACCEPTANCE:

Those are a bunch of words, but what relevance do they have to me? In my opinion, they are steps to healing. Examining where you have resistance gives valuable information. Maybe you are resisting physical pain, emotional pain, people, situations. It doesn't matter the what. What matters is if you can acquire and understand the information. I have fear around x situation, so I am resisting that experience. Is the part of you in fear able to first accept that that situation exists? Instead of "I don't want it to be this way," is that part able to accept that even if I don't want this, this is how it is right now? It is not necessarily permanent, but this is how it is right now. Once you have accepted what is, are you also ready to allow it to be, without your emotional attachment? Those two may happen at the same time, but maybe you are only accepting what is first, allowing without resistance comes later. Every person is different; every situation is different. What is possible? What can you make progress on today? Understand the simple goal—to drop resistance, allow and accept what is.

FINAL THOUGHTS

I have given lots of ideas and information in this book. Lest you fall into the trap of thinking I have it all figured out, let me tell you more about my recent past. I told of the move from Las Vegas to Phoenix and the schedule and stress and grief in that process. I did not use the tools I have written down here and others I have learned. Physically, I started to lose weight, strength, energy, and vitality. I have lost 70 pounds and have been going through joint inflammation, pain, exhaustion, and no ability to gain nutrients from the food I was eating. I have looked for solutions with supplements, epigenetic hair testing, a naturopath, blood tests, chiropractor, and medical mediums. I am beyond grateful to say that things are now starting in the right direction for me, but it has been a tough journey.

Here is the best way I have pieced together what happened. First, from a nutritional standpoint, I was not taking great care of myself. I was eating very little protein and although I like intermittent fasting, I had been eating the same thing and my pattern and timing of eating was exactly the same for several years. I was unhappy in my job with difficulties that started during the pandemic. Without specifics, some corporate decisions made my every day at work hard to get product and hard to serve customers. Personally, I had ethical problems at being put in a position of not being truthful and that did not sit well with me. Everyone is different, but it was a weight on me. I noticed the beginning of a loss of physical strength in September and October of 2023. I was let go from my job on November 1. As always, I was completely taken care of with a job offer two days later, but I was in a fear spiral. I was sitting in a soup of terror. From the outside functioning, but inside, I was frozen, totally contracted into a little ball, and shut down. I was not connecting to my body, or honoring what she asked, nay begged for. Looking back, I believe it was primarily my low vibration that caused my health decline. I say that because it was not until I truly, and in a more permanent way than a 5-minute meditation, raised my vibration that everything turned around.

The manifestation of that low vibration was that I was not absorbing nutrients from my food, so when my fat stores were empty, my body catabolized my muscles. My body was literally eating itself to stay alive. I developed habits and routines to just get through the days. I get up on weekdays and get the dogs fed. I go lie down and rest for a few minutes and that rest makes me late, so I get to the office usually 15 to 20 minutes late. As soon as I get home, after the dogs go potty, I would lie down. When I had to get up and fix dinner, I would make the easiest and fastest thing possible. I changed what I bought or cooked because I didn't feel up to standing at the stove. Instead of sautéing veggies, I only bought Brussel Sprouts or broccoli because I could use the pressure cooker, which needed no standing and tending. My eating was not good, which only added to the cascade of problems.

I did finally get sick and tired of being sick and tired. I started to look for solutions last summer. I did the hair testing and changed my diet and got some supplements. My stress hormones were all out of whack. Duh. I joined a group last fall that has been a source of so much love, challenges, and commitment. I went through some low points at the end of last year and the beginning of this one. It has only been very recently that I have seen this turn around. As always, hard experiences can be great teachers. I have seen the correlation of my health and my vibrational state. I am responsible for what vibration or frequency I am in which directly translates into vibration which makes hormones in my body. I had more than one person ask me if this was an autoimmune disease. I imagine if I went to a mainstream MD that may have been the diagnosis. But, because I believe in the power of our own minds and bodies and I do not have trust in our "healthcare" system, that was not my choice. A better label in my opinion is sick-care. Just listen to the commercials we are now subject to. Why are the side effects the same as some symptoms of what it is supposed to treat? Could it be possible that Big Pharma does not make money off products that are not trademarked like the wisdom in native cultures that have worked for centuries. Keep in mind that the "healthcare" system we use now has only been in existence for just over a hundred years. And the money and profit focus for much less than that. Companies started, just the way I think anyone who becomes a doctor starts, with the intent to yes, make money, but to help people. Johnson and Johnson started in 1886 and in the 1890's revolutionized sterile medical supplies. But, in my opinion, that great intent has been corrupted in the interest of profit. They want you to feel better, but only a little better, so you keep taking their medicine. And what does Big Pharma love more than anything? A child with disease because they will be a customer for life.

Here is my soapbox; we have poisoned our soil, our water, and our air. For convenience of the consumer, but really for the convenience of all of the manufacturing and distribution of "food," we have all the products on shelves in the middle of the grocery store. You may have heard the advice to stay around the outside of the store where you find the whole foods—produce, meat, dairy etc. In fact, around 20 years ago, I decided to change my eating style. I try to be flexible and do my best, but my primary eating choice is to have the least processing I can. I study food labels. In fact, it can become really quick. If I look at the list and it is 20 lines long, I don't even read them. Too much processing to make something that barely resembles the food it came from means I am not interested. A homemade cake has a very simple and small number of ingredients. Aside from being aware of the sugar, it is not really "bad" for you. I am speaking in general, not going into gluten sensitivity etc. I look for whole ingredients, and a short list that I can pronounce everything on the list. Just as with other ways our society places financial control on people, how in the world do we have food deserts in this country? We make it hard for folks to grow their own food too. What if all of our manicured lawns became gardens? What if on Saturday morning you didn't have to mow your lawn, but you could care for your garden and harvest food for your family.

When I was a kid, my parents would have already talked, and my mom would look for my dad's car in the driveway. She would then turn the water on to boil while Dad gathered corn from the garden. By the time he shucked it and came in, the water was ready. We would sit down to eat corn on the cob that had been growing on the stalk 30 minutes earlier. Have you ever been on a farm and eaten something that you just pulled out of the ground or off the plant? It is just delicious. Unlike anything you will ever have from the store. Think of the energy and vitality. I find Nature just amazing. Look at the cracks and crazy places where a plant will grow. Everything wants to grow and expand. So, what happens when you ingest something with that fresh life force from our Mother Earth? Our produce in the grocery store has been picked from the earth months ago, frozen or refrigerated for months so we have produce when it is not in season. It is then trucked many miles or travels halfway around the planet to land at your local store. And there is so much waste because stores have a very narrow definition of the size and shape of the produce they will use, the rest is often wasted. What if all that unused food was used as fertilizer? Sadly, it often ends up in landfills.

Why have we disempowered people? Why do people think they are not able to grow food for themselves? Even an apartment dweller can grow cherry tomatoes in a pot. There are so many possibilities, but due to cost or convenience or education, folks think they can't do it. Yes, you can! And even if you don't want to purchase the organic heirloom veggies whose seeds are much more expensive, use simple dirt and seeds. I keep my coffee grounds and my egg shells to use for fertilizer. You can even keep an earthworm house or worm bin for vermicomposting using the vegetable scrap leftovers. They will produce nutrient-rich soil you can use for fertilizer. It goes in that beautiful circle, a microcosm of our larger planet.

Back to my health journey, I also have observed a spiritual component to this. Our planet has been going through some major shifts. You can look at that from many aspects. The astrology and astronomy of some fairly unusual alignments have happened more often in the last couple of years. Seven planets aligned in February of this year. It last happened in 1982 and won't happen again until 2057. There have been many other unusual astronomical events. Also, some unique astrological events as well. Our sun goes through cycles of more and less solar activity, sending out Coronal Mass Ejections, solar wind, solar flares, and sun spots are some of the types of energy released by the sun. We have cycles known as solar minimum and solar maximum. Not surprisingly with everything else going on, we are in the peak of our solar maximum part of the cycle. That means that we are getting a ton of different frequencies of light and plasma energy coming to our planet from the sun. I know this has a physical aspect as my body is sensitive to the high energy coming in. I have correlated the days when I have no energy and feel exhausted to the days when we have a lot of energy input. This could be looked at as a physical body issue. I view it as a more spiritual energetic aspect. I have asked the spiritual questions, "Why is this happening to me? What is there for me to see or learn?" and the answer I got was, "You are making a whole new body for the next portion of your life." Wow! So, for me, I can look at any or all of the physical, emotional, and spiritual aspects and each is true. In fact, they can all be true at the same time.

Can you hear your body? Can you ask questions and quietly listen for the answers? I think it is vital to be able to discern your individual yes and no from your body. You can get so much more information. Sit quietly, connect with your body, send her or him love and peace. Make sure you are in a place you feel safe and ask if your body feels safe. Being in a safe and peaceful place is an absolute prerequisite to getting answers to questions. Developing the skill of getting quiet and listening is also required. If you have those down, then it is a matter of practice and listening. Your body wants to talk to you. For me, I have dishonored my body for so many years by not listening and driving her that I have to make sure she feels safe, seen, and honored to communicate well. Approach a conversation with your body as a sacred time; it is not a time for a casual chat. Create your space, breathe, and come from a calm place, and then see what information your body would like to tell you.

SIMPLE NOT EASY AT ITS ZENITH, ITS HIGHEST EXPRESSION

What does the zenith, the apex, the pinnacle of Simple Not Easy look like? What does it look like for me on a personal level? What does it look like on a global level?

For me, I am mostly at peace. I still have healing; I still have places to grow and expand. I often say I hope to learn something new on my last day here. I still make mistakes, I still have to apologize, but I try quickly to recover and to get to not just why did this happen and what can I learn, but why did I manifest this? Why did I create this? What is it here to show me? What is it here to teach me?

That is a huge leap. It changes the view of the world. Instead of being responsible for your response to something happening, you now take responsibility for it happening to you at all.

Wow! So, if you are that powerful, if you can create and manifest literally anything, how will you use that? I try not to look outside for why something happened. There are always reasons, but if you can see how you brought something into your life and why, what can stand in your way? You are unstoppable, and also untouchable. In other words, what can hurt you? I understand others can hurt you physically, but now I do not find much of that in my life due to my choices and how I navigate the world. You find what you are looking for.

Because you create it.

I endeavor to conduct myself on a personal level with others with respect, empathy and compassion, and free of judgement. People will always show you who they are. And usually pretty quickly. Cool! Let them be them, do what they will, and be who they are. The next choice is mine. What are my boundaries? What will I allow? Am I being conscious of my choices, my energy, my body and the feedback I am getting? This is now responding instead of reacting, and the goal is to make the choice for the highest good of all.

Not just me, which can be selfish.

Not just you, which is giving myself away.

But for the highest good, growth, and love of all. What would life look like if you use just that as a guiding principle?

Which leads to how does society look if everyone followed Simple Not Easy? I think visually of the Star Trek film where they encounter a civilization that looks totally docile, a bunch of long-haired hippies all in white clothing walking around. They have technology; they have made carefully considered choices about what they use and see on a daily basis. That's just my peaceful vision, but there is no need for all of our systems—law enforcement for example. If you treat every person you encounter with respect and compassion, nothing ever escalates to the point of physical violence. Honestly, not even verbal violence either. Conflict between people is created when both sides don't listen. If you can feel and allow the other person also to feel seen, heard, and cared about, how can you have conflict? You just see each other and look for compromise, what can you work out as a win-win for both? Or have ideas about someone who can assist in resolving what you are working out.

So, if we could all exist without conflict, what is possible? Well, everything, I imagine! We could heal each other, we could heal the air, the water, the soil, our Mother Earth herself. And then what? Could we expand to the heavens with love? Or just be and attract the right ones, the ones who are ready to see and to hear and to become. Really, everything is possible. It is a logic right from Maslow's hierarchy of needs.

The first four levels are:

- **Physiological:** Food, Shelter, Water. Your physical needs to be safe. What do you look for first if you are dropped off in the wilderness?

- **Safety:** Do I have to worry about the saber tooth tiger? Tribes or communities can provide this day-to-day safety and pre-dictability so you can relax and thrive.

- **Love and Belonging:** often with families, romantic relation-ships, though it can be many things. It has been scientifically studied what happens to human beings if they are deprived of love. Not good is the shortest way to put that outcome. We require love and connection with other people.

- **Esteem:** Maslow describes it as having two sides, one is self-es-teem. Love for oneself or self-confidence. I would put it as, I value me. The second side is having value to others. Being a loved member of a family or community that sees you and sees your contribution to them, to the tribe, to the world. My community values me. My tribe values me.

- **Self-Actualization:** This is the highest level in the hierarchy. I think most of the first four need to be at least partially met to allow you to truly thrive. Hence why I say I want to learn something new the day I leave this earth. If we are not looking for constant expansion, growth, unfoldment, why are we here?

My goals are to be present, to learn, to grow, every day. And I fall short. A Lot! And I wake up the next day with the same goal. Not Easy. For Sure. I can still beat myself up. Sometimes for a while if I feel like I deserve it. And one day, it stops feeling good. I then make a different choice. If we can all make choices based on love and who we authentically are, I think we are all unstoppable. I don't understand stepping on others to get ahead. The rising tide lifts all the boats. If I am thriving, I want to be surrounded by others who are as well. And not by isolating ourselves behind gates and fences and security. Each and every being on the planet deserves to have every opportunity to live and thrive. Supporting them takes nothing away from me.

Take that out to its logical conclusion…no war, sharing of ideas, resources, love between all people. We all are amazing individuals with so much to contribute to all of us. If there is no war, there is no military. If we think like a globe, we can stop them versus us. We don't need politics if there are no boundaries. We are all human beings. We are one. If there is no military and no politics, do we need government? Maybe if you can please keep up my roads, trash, power. Or what if we allow the people with amazing ideas who could totally change how we currently manage those things and have thriving communities in harmony for the highest good of all? I expect that each person who reads this will have their own amazing vision of what could be possible if we just made some small changes and got along with each other.

Isn't the division on the planet getting greater? I think of what I have seen in just my lifetime. We all seem to be bombarded from every source them versus us, me versus them, separate, others are scary—whatever label or category can be used. Can we just. Stop. See how it feels. Get your own guidance. I am aware this is all so utopian as not to be believed. That is OK. Find what you believe.

Standing on that belief as a firm foundation as you choose love and compassion and gratitude in your day-to-day life is a contribution to all of us.

You are a gift!

ACKNOWLEDGEMENTS

This book has been assembled from all the people and experiences that have touched my life up to this very moment.

My deepest thanks to Ann—meeting you has changed the trajectory of my life

Lil, for your thoughtful editing, wisdom, and guidance through this process

Kim, for beginning, sharing and walking beside me on this spiritual journey

Jasmine, Honey, TT, JJ, Simba, Faith, and Jasper—my beautiful teachers in dog bodies—you've each shown me what unconditional love looks like.

Thank you to Michelle for your steady support, energy, and perspective

Kara for your unwavering belief and encouragement

Jenn, Danielle, and everyone who has supported me along my health journey.

Each of you brought your kindness, wisdom, and presence that left an imprint that shaped this book in ways both seen and unseen.

To all my friends, family, and the community of souls who showed up at exactly the right times—thank you for reminding me that love and growth are collaborative acts. To every teacher, healer, and moment of challenge that pushed me forward, I offer my gratitude.

And finally, to life itself—for the lessons, the laughter, and the light that continues to guide me—this book is a reflection of all you've given.

Ellen Bone is an author based in Mesa, Arizona. Her work draws inspiration from quiet moments of awareness and the beauty found in both the seen and unseen aspects of life. When she's not writing, Ellen finds joy in the loving presence of her special angel puppy, Jasmine, and in spending time amid the red rocks and spiritual serenity of Sedona, Arizona. She enjoys leading group meditations and sound baths as pathways to stillness and deeper understanding—practices that continually inspire her words and her way of being. This is her first book.

www.ingramcontent.com/pod-product-compliance
Lightning Source LLC
Chambersburg PA
CBHW071524120626
46550CB00006B/2355